The 30,000 Mile Cat: Travels Across America

Ginnie L. Hansen

ISBN: 979-8-56-917014-2

Cover design by: Sage Sol Group LLC

AUTHOR'S NOTE

This book is based on my experiences, including traveling across the United States with my husband and our cat. Conversations are from my memory and my point of view. I used nicknames or changed names entirely to protect individual privacy. Trouble is the real name of our cat, for reasons which will become obvious. Read more about Trouble and my ongoing projects at www.the30000milecat.com.

30,000 Mile Cat Travels

CONTENTS

Follow us at the30000milecat.com and on Facebook.

FOREWORD

Standing on the mountain peak in Montana, I felt a cool breeze rifling through my hair. The sun was bright, reflecting off the snow-capped peaks that were visible in every direction under a brilliant blue sky. Directly in front of me, fields of flowers in every shade of yellow, blue, purple and red were blooming and humming with the sounds of busy bees. I laughed with joy; I couldn't imagine being anywhere else at that moment.

Sweat dripped into my eyes and as I reached up to wipe it, I snapped out of my reverie of thoughts from our summer vacation. Sitting in the front seat of our SUV, I was hot, cramped and weary after traveling for 10 days. I felt the sweat trickle down between my shoulder blades so I turned up the dial on the air conditioner. I could feel the heat of the pavement coming up through the floor of the car. My feet felt hot even though the air conditioning was blowing cold air directly on me. The thermostat said the temperature outside the car was 98 degrees Fahrenheit, but the weather app on my phone said the temperature outside felt like 105 degrees. It was hot and humid – typical August weather.

We were driving through the Southeastern United States toward Florida. This was the end of our summer and the last leg of our roundtrip from Montana, our summer home, back to Jacksonville, Florida where my husband and I work as teachers. My husband, who I call Professor, was driving; a big smile on his face as he sang along with his favorite Rush song blaring out of the radio. He enjoys driving and the intense heat of the southern summer sun blasting through the windshield didn't bother him.

I turned around to look behind me. Our cat, Trouble, was inside a large tube-shaped pet carrier that stretched across the rear seat. I peered through the black mesh of the carrier, feeling the mix of emotion that I always feel when we drive our cat across the U.S. This was our sixth trip, but the pang of guilt was the same. I adore my cat and we seem to be connected at a deep level that is hard for others to understand. I always felt conflicted; I don't feel totally comfortable when I leave her with a pet sitter, but I also feel guilty dragging her across the country.

Trouble was sitting on top of a soft sheet which formed a cushion for the ice pack we placed underneath the carrier. A battery-operated fan was clipped on top of the carrier and she stretched her face in that direction. I could see her whiskers blowing in the air.

"Is the cat okay?" Professor asked, startling me.

"She's fine; she's snoozing on her sheet," I replied while rolling my head around trying to loosen the kinks in my neck.

"Our cat has become an amazing traveler! We've made this trip six times now and each year she gets better at following the routine," Professor mused. "Do you realize that by the time we get home to Florida, we will have driven 5,200 miles on this trip alone? That's the same as driving from London, England to Beijing, China."

I nodded my head, expecting more details from Professor. He's always looking for opportunities to educate people by adding facts and statistics.

Professor smiled as he spoke. "Since we have driven this route for six years, our cat has travelled about 30,000 miles! I'm guessing that there are not too many cats who have done as much traveling as our cat. She's become a seasoned traveler."

I sat silently, thinking about our car trips from Florida to Montana. How did we get to this point? I looked again at Trouble, a colorful tortoiseshell cat who was once a stray cat sleeping in my flower garden, remembering how it all began and some of the adventures along the way.

I nodded my head. "Yes, but we had many challenging experiences during our first few years of driving from Florida to Montana. Do you remember how we couldn't get the cat to use her litter box in the car? Also, she almost jumped out of the car one time after she managed to undo the zipper on her carrier." My heart started pounding as this memory resurfaced.

"You're right; it hasn't always been easy, but now we're all veteran travelers."

As if on cue, Trouble poked her face into the mesh and grunted softly. I know my cat well; this sound means, "Are we almost there?"

"It's okay, kitty; we'll be home soon," I said, trying to reassure myself as much as the cat.

The miles continued to speed by as I thought about our experiences while traveling together and with our cat. This driving routine opened the door to unique adventures, allowing us to experience places and people that we would not have known if we had not driven across the country with our cat.

We've climbed many mountains, both real and figurative. On one memorable hike in the Rocky Mountains, we had to rescue a grandmother who was stranded after her family left her sitting on a rock in the summer heat. On another outing, we had to step carefully around a grizzly bear that was growling – a strong warning to "Keep away!"

We've experienced all kinds of weather, including record-setting hurricanes, floods and baseball-sized hail.

Yellowstone National Park has become one of our favorite destinations. On one camping trip to Yellowstone, Professor was almost trampled by bison and we nearly walked into a moose.

Through all of our trials and adventures, Trouble has been a constant companion. Now a seasoned traveler, she had a number of challenges early on, including getting lost and becoming seriously ill.

Our friends and family members have always been supportive, even while facing their own challenges. Several family members have joined us on different trips while others provided guidance and wisdom. My beloved grandmother, who has long since passed away, continues to influence my thinking through her past letters and life as a coal-miner's daughter.

This is a memoir based on my adventures while traveling with Professor and our cat, Trouble.

1 AIRPORT NIGHTMARE

The waking nightmare was always the same and I experienced a feeling of horror each time. In the nightmare, Professor and I were walking up to the airport security checkpoint holding our cat in her small, red carrier. The cat was yowling loudly, unhappy about being cooped up in the carrier when she could be home sleeping near her favorite sunny window. The security officer barked orders at us and we took the cat out of the carrier, holding tightly onto the leash. The officer turned the carrier inside and out, carefully inspecting every inch. Then he insisted on inspecting the cat.

"She's very agitated," I said, clutching the cat to my chest. "I should hold onto her." He gave me his most severe security officer look and grabbed the cat. He started combing through her fur, searching for the dangerous things that a cat might carry onto a plane. I had the urge to say, "If you see any fleas, pick them off, please," but in a rare moment of self-restraint, I kept quiet.

The security officer poked Trouble in the belly several times – something that makes her angry. Finally, she couldn't take anymore. The cat swatted at the officer's hand, raking her sharp claws across his skin and drawing blood. "Ouch!" He screamed while pulling his hand closer to examine the damage and dropping the cat who jumped off the table and ran past the security checkpoint toward the gate area.

People stopped and stared as I started running after my cat. We had not cleared security, so I heard an announcement over the loudspeaker calling additional officers to the area. Soon there were several overweight officers, not trained to run, attempting to chase after us.

I finally grabbed hold of the leash and the cat, darting into the restroom and the nearest stall. I sat down, trying to calm my cat while figuring out what to do.

My waking nightmare ended. My heart was pounding and sweat was running down my face. I stroked the cat sleeping peacefully in my lap to reassure myself that she was okay.

"We can't take the cat on a plane," I complained to Professor. I was still feeling distraught from the airport nightmare swirling around in my head. "Also, we can't leave her with a pet sitter for three months; that's too long."

"Then we will have to drive to Montana," he replied, smiling. Professor enjoys driving and was pleased to have the opportunity to drive across the country.

Sitting at the kitchen table in our home in Florida, we were discussing our plans to travel to Montana for the summer. While we were experienced travelers, we had never traveled with a pet. We were stumped on the best way to bring our cat with us to Montana.

Named Ginnie after my grandmother, I live in Jacksonville, Florida with Professor and our cat, Trouble. Professor and I moved to Florida, thinking it was a tropical paradise. We realized soon after moving to Florida, that it is in fact a tropical paradise, in-between hurricanes, floods, droughts and blazing hot summers.

Professor and I met at Temple University in Philadelphia, Pennsylvania. We both included fitness as one of our hobbies and would arrive at the gym 10 minutes before it opened. We waited together outside the door, Professor sitting on the stairs looking at his shoes while I leaned against the wall trying not to think about his broad shoulders. Professor admired my dark, wavy hair and bright blue eyes but was afraid to say more than "Hello." I was quiet and reserved, lacking confidence when meeting new people.

Eventually one of us had the nerve to say more than just "Hello" and we began working out together. As we got to know each other, we realized that we could talk about almost anything. The months drifted by until Professor had the courage to ask me out on a date. "Do English majors like to go out to the movies?" he asked.

After that first date, Professor and I were inseparable. We supported each other through many years of schooling as we both prepared to be teachers. As lifetime learners, we are curious about the world, craving knowledge and new experiences. It made sense that we committed to a life of educating others.

After we finished school, we planned a joyous wedding and got married. Over the years, we have suffered tragedies, accidents, illnesses, and arguments along with incredible joy and happiness. We often think the same thoughts, laughing as we speak an identical sentence at the same time.

Years later, Professor is an eternal optimist, whose wisdom is a rudder that keeps us moving forward on the right path. His kindness and generosity shine brightly, enveloping all who surround him. He is a teacher with a keen ability to retain all kinds of facts and statistics. Due to his extensive reading habits coupled with a photographic memory, he is consistently at the ready to advise on a wide variety of subjects. I call him Professor because he loves to regularly spout a factual tidbit, slice of history, or interesting statistic all of which can be both educational and annoying. These mini-lectures provide a colorful commentary on our adventures.

I remain reserved and am often hesitant to share personal feelings. In middle age, I have learned to take myself less seriously. I enjoy laughing and simple pleasures such as a brilliant sunset or a homemade slice of chocolate cake. Reading a good book while Professor sits on the chair next to me and Trouble sleeps in my lap brings me pure joy.

Professor and I share a passion for traveling to new places. We travel to gain fresh perspectives and experience surprise. Before we had a cat, we often took weekend trips, boarding a plane on Thursday night and returning late on Sunday. We spent the weekends exploring a park or hiking in the mountains. We have traveled around the United States visiting many national parks, including Yellowstone and Grand Teton national parks, discovering the wonders of these places. We always traveled by plane, driving in a car only after we arrived at our destination. I always believed that traveling by plane was efficient as we arrived at our destination in one day.

I enjoyed the freedom to travel on a whim. My work schedule was flexible, so even during the week I often took a break from my computer to go to one of the beaches near our home. At the beach, I relaxed while listening to the sounds of the ocean and birds. Soaking my feet in the surf, I looked for interesting shells and watched fiddler crabs dig their homes while clearing my mind of the anxieties that reside there.

Everything changed when the cat adopted us. Once Trouble, a colorful tortoiseshell cat, wandered into our garden, our lives were permanently altered. One of the most significant changes was that we decided to drive across the country, from Florida to Montana, instead of flying. This travel routine opened the door to unique adventures enabling us to experience places and people that we would not have known otherwise.

It all resulted from the fact that we could not bear to leave our beloved cat behind. I have always been self-reliant, trying to manage life's challenges on my own or with Professor's help. Having a cat meant I had to change my ways, learning to rely on others for advice and assistance. It was not easy for me to ask for help, but my friends and family rose to the task. My parents, Mom and Dad, allowed us to take over their house in Ohio with our cat and supplies. They cheerfully entertained Trouble while Professor and I recovered from long days of driving or went shopping to replenish our supplies.

I found inspiration and support from other family members. My grandmother, whose relationship I treasured, provided the inspiration to tell many of the stories in this book. Hers was a colorful life, grounded in selfless love, always putting others first. Grandma's spirit lives in the many cards, letters and photos that she sent me throughout her life. Her stories have become mine to share.

My two younger sisters, Shirley and Kathy, provided support from their experience with their families and pets. Our shared memories from trips taken as a family when we were younger infused humor into my travel stories.

Our cat Trouble is now a valued family member, but this was not always the case. Trouble has a charming face which defies her precocious personality. The colors on her face – black, white, and tan create an adorable rainbow mask of color, contrasting with her white chest and black legs. When we take her to the vet, she is regularly admired by perfect strangers for her beauty and sweet demeanor. "Oh, what a pretty cat! She's so sweet," they say.

Trouble is very vocal, making all kinds of sounds to communicate her wants and needs. Cats have the ability to make more than 100 sounds; only birds make more sounds than cats. Trouble has all of these sounds mastered, including yowling, meowing, chirping, chattering, hissing, growling and purring. Over the years, we have learned to understand these sounds and to communicate with our cat.

A social cat who demands a lot of attention, Trouble will run to the door to greet visitors in our house. She purrs happily as people pet her and rub behind her ears. She charms them by rubbing against their legs and licking their hands. People often ask, "This cat is so friendly. Why did you name her Trouble?"

"Well, let me tell you how she got her name," I respond. "It's a long story."

Like most cats, Trouble clings to her routine, and suffers severe anxiety when her schedule is interrupted. She expresses her displeasure in a number of ways, and this often includes making some type of mess for her owners to clean up. The mess may be in the form of shredded fabric on the living room furniture, or using something other than her litter box to do her business.

So, when Professor and I decided to drive 2,600 miles from Florida to Montana and then another 2,600 miles back to Florida, we were not sure how we would travel with our adorable and challenging cat. All we knew for certain was that it would be complicated. However, we figured it couldn't be any more complex than when, before Trouble entered our lives, we were indoctrinated into the hazards of Florida's hurricane culture.

2 ESCAPING HURRICANE FLOYD

Professor and I were looking for storage bins that we could use for our trip across the country. In one bin, we found a photo from a dinner party at my Great Aunt Betty's house. The photo was taken the day after Hurricane Floyd went up the east coast of Florida causing a major disruption in our lives. We sat down in the sunroom with cold glasses of water to cool off and reminisce about our early experiences in Florida. Trouble jumped up on the chair next to me, purring and intently watching the birds in the birdfeeders.

We moved from Pennsylvania to Florida in the middle of a hot summer, renting an apartment in downtown Jacksonville. Professor drove from Pennsylvania to Florida in a Chevrolet Corsica with a broken air conditioner. Repairing the air conditioner was expensive and since we were living on one income, he didn't want to spend the money to have it fixed.

In the summer, temperatures in Florida average above 90 degrees Fahrenheit with the humidity making it feel like over 100 degrees. I could not understand how he could commute to work for 30 minutes in a car with no air conditioning. When I asked how he was tolerating the heat, he replied, "It's okay, I just leave the windows down." Professor returned from work with his sweaty shirt plastered to his skin and his tie askew, but he didn't complain. It's not in his nature to complain.

When we moved to Florida, we had only been married for a few years. I remember thinking about our wedding vows, "I promise to listen to you, laugh with you, encourage and understand you, through all the changes in our lives." I had to keep reminding myself about the laughing and encouragement part throughout our first years of living in Florida.

Professor and I grew up in the northeastern part of the United States, where summer days can be hot, but the evening brings cooler air. The intense heat and humidity of the Florida summer felt unbearable. Even with the air conditioning set on a cold temperature, I still felt the humidity and hot sun pounding on the roof of the apartment building. Professor worked long hours and I was alone all day in the apartment. I didn't know anyone and had not yet found a job. I felt like a captive in the apartment, not wanting to venture out to face the wall of heat that hit me when I stepped out the door. I wondered daily why we had moved away from our family and house in Pennsylvania with our flower and vegetable gardens, giant hickory nut tree and cool evening breezes.

Hurricane Floyd interrupted everything. The pictures on the television showed the hurricane with 110 mile-per-hour winds coming up the east coast of Florida. At the time, Floyd was the one of the strongest storms to threaten the east coast of the United States. In the following years, we would experience more record-breaking storms.

Watching the meteorologists on television talking about the size and intensity of the storm, with a projected path that included Jacksonville, we started to panic. We were aware of hurricanes when we moved to Florida, remembering the tragic loss of life and devastation from Hurricane Andrew. Prior to this, we naively thought hurricanes only impacted Miami.

The local meteorologists predicted that Hurricane Floyd could hit Jacksonville straight on. Mandatory evacuation orders were issued for areas along the coast and it was strongly suggested that people in the rest of the city evacuate. With pictures of the flattened landscape that remained after Hurricane Andrew in our minds, we were terrified. Most of our worldly goods were in storage, so we quickly packed a couple of suitcases, put the bikes on the car and locked up the apartment.

We called my Great Aunt Betty in Mount Dora, Florida asking if we could stay with her and my Great Uncle Nick. "We will be there in 2 hours," I said, confidently.

"We look forward to your visit," Great Aunt Betty replied, cheerfully.

Professor drove our car out of the apartment complex parking lot and then stopped. There were cars as far as we could see – in front of us, behind us, backed up onto the off-ramps and on-ramps for the main highway. We were stuck in the largest traffic mess that I had ever seen as everyone tried to leave Florida to get out of Floyd's path.

"It might take a little longer than two hours," Professor spoke slowly. He's always optimistic and his positive nature balances out my tendency to expect the worst.

"If we even get there," I replied, my anxiety escalating. I am a realist, believing that things often work out for the best, but disasters can happen. This means that I constantly worry about what might happen in the next minute, hour, day and week.

We never considered turning around and going back to the apartment. Being new to the area and hurricanes, we trusted the forecast from the local meteorologists, believing that evacuation was our only choice. We sat in traffic for hours, creeping along at 10 miles-per-hour. At least Professor had the foresight to fill up the gas tank. We passed by many stations with "No Gas" signs and cars lining the road with empty gas tanks.

Sitting in the car, creeping along in the traffic, we anxiously listened to the storm updates on the local radio station. Tropical rains started pounding the car and I turned up the volume so we could hear every word of the news on the storm. The scheduled radio program was constantly interrupted by weather-related watches and warnings from the National Hurricane Center. "The National Weather Service has issued a hurricane warning for St. Johns County, Florida." That was us. Stuck in traffic, we were also now in the path of the outer bands of the hurricane, bringing heavy rain, high winds and flooding.

The radio blared another warning. "The National Weather Service has issued a tornado warning for St. Johns County. A tornado has been spotted in the area of Route 16." I looked up at the street sign on the corner ahead of us. The sign said, "Route 16."

"Great, now we are in the path of a tornado," I mumbled, as the seeds of panic began to grow within me at an accelerated pace. I could feel my chest tightening as my anxiety took over. I was trying my best not to alarm Professor, who was starting to look weary from driving the car at a glacial pace through the unyielding traffic jam.

The tornado warnings advised people to "seek shelter." In a matter of seconds, countless scenarios unwound in my mind, generating more questions than answers. *Where could we seek shelter while sitting in unmoving traffic on a country road surrounded by farm fields?* Unfortunately, there was only one answer – there was no shelter. We had no choice but to remain in our car and hope, with every fiber of our being, that we were not in the path of the tornado.

The intensity of the rain and wind increased. The noise was so loud that I had to turn up the volume of the radio even higher. "A flood watch has been issued for St. Johns County." Now I was worried about rain, wind, tornadoes and flooding. I slouched in my seat, pulling on my seatbelt to tighten it. I was so frightened that I could only focus on my labored breathing and the tension in my neck. I stayed quiet, trying not to bother Professor who was now also feeling stressed. His hands gripped the steering wheel and he slouched forward in his seat. We were captives with no place to go to escape the situation. All we could do was sit in the car, watching the traffic and waiting to see what would happen with the hurricane.

We made it to Mount Dora after sitting in traffic and battling the weather for eight hours. The trip would normally take two hours. Professor and I were both mentally and physically exhausted. I sat silently in the passenger seat as a sense of relief began to creep into my body. Professor hummed his favorite tune, already recovering from the stressful experience.

As our car pulled into the driveway, Great Aunt Betty and Great Uncle Nick came out to greet us. "We were worried about you!" Great Uncle Nick exclaimed while giving me a big hug.

We were relieved to be there and felt safer being with family. While Professor and Great Uncle Nick were bringing the luggage into the house, Great Aunt Betty was rushing around filling up containers with water. "I wonder if we have enough water," she mumbled quietly, not realizing that I could hear her.

I felt terrible as I realized that we had arrived at their house in the middle of a horrendous storm with no extra water or storm supplies. All of the stores were closed and it was too dangerous to be on the roads. Professor and I had been more worried about packing our worldly belongings such as our beach gear and bikes and didn't bring any bottled water or canned food. We had only called Great Aunt Betty yesterday which meant she did not have enough time to plan for extra supplies. Writing these words years later, I still feel guilty for putting such pressure on two elderly people.

Discussing this the next day, Professor offered a positive perspective. He said, "They enjoyed seeing us," and "Everything worked out fine." He was right, of course. After the storm passed, having only a minor impact on Florida, we had a dinner party including friends and relatives. The photo of everyone sitting at the table, smiling, is a reminder of how it was essential to have family whom we could rely upon in an emergency.

We returned to our apartment in Jacksonville to find a light blinking furiously on our answering machine. Our family members in New York and Pennsylvania saw the news on the hurricane and were worried, so they left many messages. I called my parents to let them know we were all right. Mom, a retired nurse, had all kinds of questions about our health. Dad, a retired insurance agent, wanted to know if we had any damage to our property.

After reassuring Mom and Dad that we were fine and had no damage from the hurricane, I called my grandmother. Grandma was one of my favorite people and we usually talked on the phone once a week. She was not worried. "I prayed for you and knew that you would be okay," she said, softly. Grandma lived a faith-based existence and alleviated her worries about others by praying for them.

After talking to our family members, we returned to our dreary apartment feeling drained from the experience. This was my third month living in Florida, a place I had moved to because of the weather, and up to this point the weather had been dreadful.

3 THE CAT ADOPTS US

Spring comes early in Florida. On a bright January day, I began writing packing lists for our trip to Montana in May. Soon I had headache from thinking about packing and traveling, so I went out to the garden to pull weeds. The neighbor's cat, a bright orange and cream tabby called Allie Cat, came out from under a bush to greet me. As I rubbed the cat's head, I remembered when Trouble first showed up in our yard.

Some years ago, on a warm fall afternoon, I took a break from gardening, standing up to wipe the sweat from my brow. Admiring my handiwork in the raised flower bed, I saw a strange cat wander into the yard. We have seen many animals walk down the stone path through the yard into the forest behind our house including cats, dogs, deer, armadillos, raccoons, rabbits, opossums and tortoises. The colorful tortoiseshell cat trotted toward me and I stared at her charming face.

The cat greeted me by licking my hand and soaked up all of the attention that I could give her. I patted her on the head and went back to my gardening. She followed me all around the yard, rubbing against my legs and then sitting in the shade snoozing and watching me work through half-open eyelids. I had never seen this cat in the neighborhood, but she looked healthy, so I assumed she belonged to a neighbor. I played with her, waving a weed in front of her as she swatted at it and then went back to pulling weeds, not giving any more thought to the cat.

From that day on, every time I stepped out of the house, the cat was there to greet me. She was playful and mischievous, always looking for a game of chasing butterflies or swatting at my shoelaces. The cat was very vocal, and we learned to understand each other. If Professor and I were sitting in the sunroom, she would sit outside the door and yowl until we gave her some attention. She was very devilish, chasing salamanders, tree frogs, bugs and anything else that moved. Sometimes she would hide behind a bush and jump out at me as I walked through the yard. I started saying "Here comes trouble," when I saw the cat in our yard. As often happens with pets, the name chose her and we called her Trouble from that day on.

The neighbor's son saw me playing with the cat one day and came into our yard to pet her. "Are you playing with our cat?" he asked. I assumed she belonged to the neighbor, but I never saw her go near their house. She continued to follow me around the yard, talking to me and demanding attention.

Trouble filled a space in my heart left there by other pet cats. I always enjoyed being around cats, petting their silky fur and relaxing to the hum of their purring. When I was a child, my family had several cats and I have fond memories of those cats. Harry was my first cat. I named him after one of my favorite children's books, *Take a Nap, Harry* by Mary Chalmers. In my five-year-old mind, he looked just like the cat in the book. He was a sweet-natured cat with a shiny black coat. We got Harry as a kitten when we lived in New Jersey and he traveled with us when my family moved to the Mohawk Valley in Upstate New York.

The cat's name caused some problems in our new home in New York. The neighbor's name was also Harry. The neighbor was not friendly and not fond of cats. When Mom yelled "Harry" out the back door to call the cat, she feared she might disturb Harry, the neighbor.

Harry didn't thrive in our new home. He would go out wandering and not always come back for his breakfast. He was hit by a car on a busy street one night. My parents were at a party so the babysitter answered the door. A neighbor was holding Harry, who was gravely injured. The babysitter laid him on a blanket on the couch. He didn't make it through the night.

My sisters and I stood silently with tears in our eyes as Mom and Dad buried our beloved cat in a shoebox in our backyard. This was one of my first experiences with loss and the memories are still vivid and painful.

Webster was another family cat. Dad and I found Webster at the local Humane Society and brought him home as a present for Mom on her birthday. He had a bold personality and lots of energy. On his first night in the house, he knocked over an antique vase which cracked in half as it hit the floor. Mom was infuriated and insisted that we return the cat to the Humane Society, but the cat had already worked his way into our hearts.

Professor met Webster on his first visit to my childhood home in Upstate New York. He slept on the couch in the family room in the basement. During the night, he heard the cat creeping around the room and walking on the beams in the ceiling. Professor drifted off to sleep only to be awakened in a panic when Webster jumped from the ceiling down onto Professor's chest.

Professor was very kind and never mentioned that he didn't like cats because he was allergic to them.

When Trouble started visiting our yard, I remembered the joys and tribulations of owning a cat. When I saw her adorable face, my heart softened toward her and everyone around me. I felt more relaxed and able to face the challenges of life. Pets bring tremendous joy and unconditional love into our lives. I also realized that pet ownership is a daily responsibility. Pets need to be fed and cared for throughout the day and trips to the veterinarian can be expensive.

Professor's family never had a cat since he and his sister are allergic to cats. His family had a dog, Pepper, who was beloved, so Professor understood what it meant to have a pet. Still, he was biased against cats. "I don't like cats; they trigger my asthma," he would remind me when we saw a cat in our neighborhood.

When Professor and I discussed having a pet, he would say, "We can't have a pet because we travel a lot."

Since the neighbor's son claimed Trouble as his cat, we didn't worry about taking care of her. She seemed to be well-fed and her shiny coat and long whiskers indicated good health.

That summer, we went on vacation to the Pacific Northwest for two weeks. We returned from our trip to hot, dry weather; Florida was in a severe drought. As Professor pulled the car into the driveway, we could see that our grass had turned yellow and the flowers by the mailbox had been toasted brown by the hot Florida sun and lack of moisture.

As soon as I stepped out of the car, Trouble hobbled over to me – very slowly. She was weak, thin and dehydrated. She mewled softly like a kitten; a pathetic sound compared to her usual boisterous yowling. I dropped my luggage and ran into the house, immediately giving the cat a bowl of water and a can of tuna. She quickly devoured the tuna and the water then weaved between my legs, looking for more. I fed her until she was content and sleeping in the shade on the side of the house.

After that, Trouble began showing up on our front step every morning for breakfast. I gave her a bowl of food and then sent her on her way, but she always came back the next morning. She continued to follow me around the yard when I was gardening and doing chores.

Our friend Elaine, a volunteer at the local animal shelter offered some advice. "Cats will change homes if they're unhappy." I'm not sure if this was the case, but it was apparent that I was the only person feeding and caring for Trouble. As soon as I opened the front door in the morning, she would jump up and rub against my legs, yowling loudly until I gave her some food.

Professor adored Trouble and would play with her when he was working in the yard, but he made it clear that she was not allowed in the house. Each time Professor saw me feeding or playing with Trouble, he would adamantly remind me, "We can't have a cat. You know that I'm allergic to cats and we travel a lot."

"I know," I replied, while scooping food into the cat's dish. "I'm just giving her a little bit of food to keep her healthy." This continued for several months, until the weather changed.

That winter, we had a cold snap with temperatures below freezing for several nights. I worried about Trouble's safety but was afraid to bring her inside the house. When I was a kid, we had a flea infestation in our family room and I remember being bitten by hundreds of fleas while trying to watch television. I imagined that this cat had fleas crawling all over her. We put Trouble in the sunroom with an old blue wool blanket folded up in a lawn chair. When I showed her the chair, she sniffed it and pawed at the blanket.

Busy covering my plants and fruit trees to protect them from the frost, I didn't check on the cat until late in the evening. Opening the door to the sunroom and looking at the chair, I could see the blue blanket but not the cat. I was concerned about her because the temperature was already below freezing.

"Trouble! Come here, kitty! Come inside!" I yelled loudly. At the sound of my voice, her face poked out from under the blanket. She had molded the blanket into an igloo and crawled inside it. I stuck my hand inside her little nest; it was very warm. I went to bed knowing she was safe and warm.

After the bitter cold weather, we slipped into a routine where Trouble was eating and sleeping in the sunroom. Each day I left fresh food, water and a clean litter box in the sunroom. She seemed to already know how to use the litter box. I still was not sure if Trouble belonged to the neighbor, but they never called her or came looking for her.

Professor constantly reminded me, "We can't have a cat." Even as he said it, he continued to get more attached to Trouble. She was always friendly and ready to play. When we were out in the yard she would run and jump and play like a kitten, chasing anything that moved, including my feet. When Trouble got bored with the garden, she would demand some human attention. Finally worn out, she would curl up in the blue wool blanket on the chair and nap contentedly. I was pleased to see her there and enjoyed her company. It felt like she was a member of our family.

One night, Professor and I were sitting at the kitchen table finishing dinner. I could see into the sunroom where a blur of black and brown fur was sitting by the bowl of cat food. "The cat's returned for her dinner," I said to Professor, eating another bite of my pasta.

Professor nodded his head in agreement, although the look on his face was a reminder that he did not approve of me feeding the cat in the sunroom. Looking more carefully, I noticed that the animal's movements were different from a cat. I walked over to the screen door and found myself face-to-face with a large raccoon. The raccoon sat by the screen door staring at me, as if to say "Why are you interrupting my dinner?"

I yelled "Shoo!" The raccoon ran away but was persistent, coming back each night looking for more food.

After the raccoon incident, I allowed Trouble into the house. I left the screen door to the house open so she could come inside to eat her food and nap in a soft chair. While I was working at home during the day, the house was very quiet. I enjoyed the solitude and the lack of noise allowed me to focus on my work. When I needed a break from work, Trouble would sit at my feet, purring and licking my hand as I scratched her back. I could feel my body relax and tension from work would melt away. At night, when Professor was home, she slept in the sunroom.

Trouble came home for her meals right on schedule. While she ate dinner, I closed the doors so she would be safe and the raccoons could not eat her food. At first, Trouble didn't like being kept inside. She enjoyed her freedom and wanted to be able to commune with the other animals in the yard. She ate her food quickly and then tried to dart out the door before I closed it.

One night, I found Trouble sitting on the patio staring at a large opossum. The opossum was sitting perfectly still, staring back at the cat. I panicked, picturing the opossum tearing the cat apart with her sharp teeth and claws.

"Trouble, come inside," I said gently, trying not to upset the opossum. The cat just sat there, staring at the opossum. I made loud noises to scare the opossum; it didn't move. Eventually the opossum went on her way and Trouble came inside while I quickly closed the door behind her. Later, I learned that cats and opossums often get along. Trouble and the opossum were enjoying each other's company.

We continued the charade with Professor reminding me that "We can't keep a cat," while I continued taking care of Trouble as if she was our cat. She continued to eat in the house and sleep in the sunroom at night. The door to the sunroom stayed open so she could come and go freely during the day.

The open sunroom attracted a lot of attention from other creatures. Each time I opened the sliding glass door, I looked carefully around the floor before stepping gingerly into the sunroom. One day, Trouble was standing steadfast by a large flower pot. Crouched in hunting position, she stared at the base of the flower pot. "What are you looking at, kitty?" I asked. In response, the cat started batting at something, moving her right paw quickly around the base of the flower pot. Looking more closely, I saw a pygmy rattlesnake curled around the base of the pot.

"Trouble, what are you doing?" I screamed as the cat played with the snake, swatting at it with her paw. Snakes are not my favorite creatures, but they are good for the garden, eating lots of bugs and mosquitoes. Mosquitoes are ferocious during the summer so I try not to disturb snakes. This was different; a pygmy rattlesnake is poisonous. I did not have a way to safely catch the snake, so I found a garden shovel and killed it. As I disposed of the dead snake, I felt guilty about killing it. I reminded myself that even though a pygmy rattlesnake is only somewhat dangerous to humans, it can be deadly to a small cat.

Once again, the weather changed our routine. During Hurricane Season, which starts on June 1 and ends on December 1, local news websites publish storm preparation checklists. One of the items on the list is "Keep pets safe." I stared at the words on the list. Trouble wasn't officially our pet; I still thought of her as a stray cat that I was feeding. However, after living for a number of years in Florida, we had plenty of experience with tropical storms. I could picture the trees bending in the wind, branches breaking off and hitting the ground. The rain would pound the roof of the house – a noise so loud that I would have to turn up the music on my player to drown out the sound.

A little cat would not be safe outside during a severe storm. There was no other option; she had to come inside the house. "We have to bring the cat inside during the storm," I said to Professor, speaking in an even tone, trying to make it sound like an everyday task.

"Ginnie, you know that I'm allergic to cats. Trouble can't come inside the house. The cat could trigger an asthma attack," he replied swiftly, annoyed that I would even mention it.

"Well, we can't leave her outside and the sunroom is not safe in tropical storm winds. The garage gets water on the floor and it's too hot in there, especially if the electricity and the air conditioning go off. She has to come inside the house." I took a big breath, and held on to it because I was very worried about this cat who had become my little buddy. I worked on my arguments before having the conversation, knowing that Professor's big heart would be soft when it came to the cat's safety.

Professor relented and we brought the cat inside the house the day before the storm. Trouble quickly found the softest blanket in the house, curled up on it and went to sleep. Professor coughed and sneezed until he took some allergy medicine. Then we all hunkered down until the storm passed.

Tropical Storm Fay caused a lot of flooding in Jacksonville, but compared to other storms, the damage was minor. I got up early on Saturday after the storm to teach an eight-hour class. I fed the cat and kissed Professor who was still sleeping.

Arriving home at 5:30 p.m., I threw my books and teaching materials on the floor. I was exhausted from the storm and teaching an 8-hour class and desperately needed a nap. Looking across the living room, I saw the primary nap spot in the house, the couch, was already taken. Professor was stretched out on the couch with his mouth open, breathing deeply while making a slight snoring sound. The afternoon sunlight was glinting off his bald head. Sitting on top of his broad chest, staring at me with a smug look on her face, was the cat. Trouble, the stray cat who did not like to be held or restrained in any way, was snoozing on Professor's chest.

This was shocking. As a stray cat, Trouble was always very skittish. She did not like to be held and would not sit on my lap. When she walked across the room, she stayed close to the wall or the couch. I had to be very careful when I reached for her; she did not like quick movements. One time I reached for her too quickly and she almost scratched my eye out.

Professor's eyes blinked open and he stared at the cat on his chest. He sneezed violently, but Trouble didn't move. She was relaxed and perfectly content. No one spoke; we just looked at the cat who seemed to know exactly what to do to get what she wanted. It was like she was telling us, "This is where I belong."

Mom and Dad came to visit us in early December, after the end of hurricane season. They enjoyed going to the beach and swimming in the ocean. They also enjoyed spending time with our cat. Trouble followed Dad around the house, waiting for him to sit down so she could jump in his lap. Once the cat settled into Dad's lap, the pair would take a nap with both of them snoring.

In the evening when we all sat in the living room reading our books, Trouble settled on the back of the armchair behind Mom's head. She buried her nose in Mom's curly hair, while trying to keep her nose warm. In the photo that I took that day, it looks like Trouble is smelling Mom's hair.

While watching Trouble interact with my parents, I also thought about Grandma. Grandma never met Trouble, but I imagined that they would be good friends. Grandma adored all animals.

I was amazed at how quickly Trouble settled into becoming a house cat. It was official; Trouble had adopted us.

4 RIVER CITY

While cleaning out the garage and looking for bins to take on our trip to Montana, I found the life vests that we used with our kayak. We had given the kayak to friends who lived near the water, so I took the vests inside the house and put them on the pile of goods for donation to a local charity. Trouble walked over to investigate and started chewing on the strap that secures the vest. She loves to play with string or anything that looks like string.

"What is Trouble chewing on?" Professor looked up from reading the newspaper.

"The life vests that we used when we had the kayak." I picked the cat up and put the vests inside a bag. Trouble will eat almost anything and I worried that she would swallow some of the fabric from the strap.

"The kayak! I haven't thought about that for a while. We had great adventures with the kayak. Do you remember when the fish jumped into your lap?" Professor laughed.

I smiled as the memories came back to me. "Yes, I remember. It was a crazy day."

We reminisced about our adventures with the kayak. After Hurricane Floyd, we were still living in an apartment. We decided that we needed a new sport to get us out of the apartment on the weekends. Often called the River City, the history and development of Jacksonville has revolved around the water including the St. Johns River, the Atlantic Ocean and the Intracoastal Waterway. Water sports are very popular so we went shopping for a kayak.

We bought a bright yellow two-person kayak which weighed 90 pounds. The store employees put the kayak on the roof rack of our small car and we drove to our apartment, chatting excitedly about all of the places where we could take the kayak. There was only one problem. We forgot that our apartment was on the second floor.

Taking the 90-pound, 15-foot kayak off the roof of the car took most of our strength, so Professor and I sat on the stairs to rest before trying to carry the kayak up to the apartment. Professor took this opportunity to give a history lesson. He is passionate about history and enjoys educating others. I listened carefully since we were new to Jacksonville and I wanted to understand the city. Also, I needed the rest.

Professor spoke slowly and carefully since he was still learning the history of our new home. "The waterways around Jacksonville are an important part of the history. Jacksonville was established by British colonists in the late 18th century and was originally called 'Cow Ford' in recognition of the ford used to cross cattle over the St. Johns River. Isaiah Hart established the City of Jacksonville, naming it after Florida Territory Governor Andrew Jackson, in 1822. The St. Johns River flows from south to north and empties into the Atlantic Ocean east of downtown Jacksonville. This is right near Kathryn Abbey Hanna Park which is one of our favorite beaches."

After the brief history lesson, we picked up the kayak and started up the stairs. I went up the stairs first, walking backwards while holding one end of the kayak. Professor stood on the lower stairs shouting directions while holding the bulk of the weight of the boat. An hour later, we put the kayak on the second-floor landing. We sat on top of the kayak with sweat pouring down our faces. I was wondering what we were thinking when we bought this cumbersome boat.

I imagined tenants in other apartments peeking out of their windows and muttering to themselves, "Crazy people!" At that moment they would have been right. When the store manager said the two-person kayak was a "true test of a marriage," I thought he was referring to the challenge of paddling the boat. Getting the boat off the car and into our apartment was far more difficult.

Eventually, we developed a routine for maneuvering the kayak on the stairs, on and off the car and in the water. We took the kayak out on the water every weekend. One memorable fall afternoon, we paddled slowly through the waves on the St. Johns River, enjoying the cool weather which was a welcome break after a long, hot and humid summer. Sitting in the front of the kayak while Professor sat in the rear, steering, I lifted my face to the sun, feeling its warmth as the light breeze ruffled my hair. A large alligator went motoring by and we both stopped paddling, sitting silently in awe and a bit of fear until it was out of view.

I turned around to talk to Professor and saw him staring at the Buckman Bridge, the three-mile-long bridge spanning the St. Johns River. I could tell from his intense expression that he was thinking about the connections between the river and the growth of the city. The bridge is one of seven bridges in the city and hundreds of thousands of cars cross it every day. Most people who pass through Jacksonville cross over the St. Johns River. Many travelers are heading to points further south such as St. Augustine, Daytona Beach and Orlando.

Professor had been reading more about the river's history. "The St. Johns River has supported humans for thousands of years. The Timucuan Indians called the St. Johns River 'Welaka' which means River of Lakes. During Spanish rule, which began in the 1500's with the arrival of Ponce de Leon in nearby St. Augustine, the river was renamed to Rio de San Juan – St. Johns River in English. The famous naturalist, William Bartram, explored the St. Johns River in the late 1700's, going upriver near the headwaters. Ironically, we lived on Bartram Avenue in Philadelphia and then moved near Bartram Highway south of Jacksonville, Florida."

As I listened to Professor's mini-lecture, I looked across the river. I could see Naval Air Station Jacksonville where I had begun teaching classes on the weekend. Navy bases are an important part of Jacksonville's history. During the World War II period, the military constructed three massive bases within the city limits, making it the third largest military complex in the United States. Although one of those bases has since closed, Mayport Naval Station and Naval Air Station Jacksonville are still integral to the city's economy and culture.

My attention returned to the river. In the fall, large schools of mullet fish can be seen leaping several feet out of the water. As we talked, we watched the mullets shooting out of the water and arching back into it with a smooth dive. I was fascinated. I didn't realize that fish could leap out of the water like that.

Suddenly, a mullet leapt out of the water near the kayak and landed in my lap. I started yelling and shifting around on my seat, trying to get the flapping, wet fish out of my lap.

Professor shouted, "What's wrong?" and "Stop rocking the boat!"

"There's a fish on my lap!"

"What?"

"A fish! On my lap!"

"Calm down, Ginnie. If you keep rocking like that you will tip the boat over." Professor is calm even in an emergency.

I didn't respond because I was desperately trying to catch the large fish flopping around in my lap, but fish scales are slippery and the fins are sharp. The mullet finally fell into the bottom of the boat, continuing to flop around. I sat staring at it, wondering what I should do next.

"Throw the fish out of the boat," Professor directed.

It was good advice, but I could not hold onto the fish long enough to pick it up. I continued staring at it, feeling sorry for the fish which was out of its environment. Fish scales were scattered on the bottom of the boat.

A nearby fisherman saw the chaos and rowed his boat next to ours. Laughing, he scooped the mullet up in his net and took the fish home for dinner. Professor and I returned to our apartment, exhausted from the adventure.

Eventually we moved out of the apartment and settled in a small house in suburban Jacksonville. The house was in Fruit Cove, an area known for fruit orchards including oranges. The kayak had its own spot in the corner of the garage. Once we moved into the house, we did not use the kayak as much since we were busy working long hours. We managed to take several weekend trips to Ocala National Forest, Everglades National Park, Blue Spring State Park and Biscayne Bay. We saw lots of wildlife including great blue herons, egrets, turtles, dolphins and whales. The diversity of wildlife was one of our favorite aspects of life in Florida.

On rare occasions, we saw a manatee. We felt privileged since the West Indian Manatees, or sea cows, are protected by law as an endangered species. Known as the gentle giants of the sea, they are placid by nature and graceful swimmers. Manatees are large, gray mammals with two front flippers and a flat paddle-shaped tail. They have a long snout with whiskers and a wrinkled face. The average adult is about 10 feet long weighing 800 to 1,200 pounds. Manatees are relatives of elephants and the similarity is apparent in photos.

Each year, many manatees are killed or injured by watercraft collisions, ingesting fish hooks, litter or by becoming entangled in traps or fishing lines. Many organizations are working to help save this important creature.

After living in Jacksonville for a few years we learned more about the history of the city. Jacksonville has grown dramatically in the 21st century and now includes a diverse population. However, a particularly dark period occurred in the 1950's and 1960's during the fight for civil rights. The era was marked by protests and civil unrest. In 1960, a violent mob attacked peaceful protesters at a local lunch counter. This infamous episode, now called "Ax Handle Saturday," marked one of the turning points in the area's civil rights movement. This history is acknowledged annually and can be experienced in person along the African-American Heritage Trail in Jacksonville.

Our professional lives continued to get busier, but on weekends we appreciated the nature around us by watching birds and animals in our yard, laughing at dolphins in the ocean and getting upset when a bald eagle hunted birds in our feeders. Life settled down to a steady routine until Trouble appeared in our garden.

5 LOST CAT

One afternoon, Professor and I were sitting in the sunroom discussing our summer travel plans, enjoying cool weather and watching the birds in our feeders. We have several types of bird feeders and enjoy watching the cardinals, blue jays, woodpeckers, chickadees, hummingbirds and nuthatches in the yard. Watching the birds build their nests in our trees and then bring their offspring to the feeders is relaxing and allows us to connect to the natural world.

Trouble was still adjusting to life as a house cat. She had strong urges to go outside, especially in the early spring. This was one of those days. She longed to be running around in the garden, chasing lizards, frogs and bugs, and stalking birds in the birdhouses.

While we tried to relax, Trouble sat by the door to the yard, crying mournfully. "No, kitty," I said, patiently. "You can't go out." She understood what I said and stopped howling. She jumped on top of the nearby picnic table, sulking while her tail moved slowly back and forth.

Trouble looked down at my sunglasses sitting next to her on the table. She stretched out her left paw and lightly tapped the sunglasses, moving them across the table. She continued pushing them to the edge of the table until they fell onto the floor. Then she looked at me as if to say, "If I don't get my way, I will find a way to get even." I should have been angry, but instead I laughed. Our cat is always inventing new tricks and games.

After tropical storm Fay, Trouble became an indoor cat. This was a challenging time as we adjusted to the new routine of having a cat in the house. Typical of a cat, she expected us to adjust to her schedule. At 4 a.m., she would come into the bedroom, making a shrill howling noise. Jolted awake by the sound of distress, my heart pounding, I worried that she was ill.

"What's the matter, Trouble?" I would yell, jumping out of bed and running to her side. She would run to her food bowl and look up at me with sad, expectant eyes.

"It's not time to eat, kitty," I would say, trying to be patient, stroking her back to relax her before I stumbled back to bed.

"What's the matter with the cat?" Professor would mumble, half asleep.

"She's hungry," I would say as I laid my head back down on the pillow. Within a few minutes, I would hear another loud yowl. I need my sleep and the constant disruption was making it difficult for me to function during the day.

After several weeks of being awakened at 4 a.m. by the cat, I was tired, cranky and frustrated. I adored Trouble, but she was interfering with my sleep. I was barely functioning; my productivity at work was falling and my patience with Professor and colleagues fluctuated between little to none.

Desperate for more sleep, I bought several books on animal behavior and training cats, including *Animals Make Us Human* by Temple Grandin and *Guide to a Well-Behaved Cat* by Phil Maggitti. I learned to understand my cat's behavior and how to train her to be a well-behaved house cat. It took time and lots of patience, but eventually I was able to train Trouble to be quiet in the morning.

Now when she feels hungry and I'm sleeping, she stands by my head and looks at me. I wake up, aware of the cat standing next to my pillow, and look at her with one eye open. "Settle down, Trouble," I say, gently. She walks to the foot of the bed and sits quietly until the alarm goes off. Hearing the alarm, she moves closer to my head, purring in my ear, and allowing me to hear her stomach growling. She doesn't make any other noise, although she may butt my head with her head or lick my face. Most days she waits patiently for me to get up so we can start the day together.

Keeping Trouble inside the house during the evening was also an ongoing challenge. Once the sun went down, she was ready to go outside and chase all of the creatures that come out at night in the dense woods in Florida. At dusk, she would stand by the door, crying pitifully.

"You can't go out, kitty. It's too dangerous," I explained. There were rumors of dogs and cats disappearing in the neighborhood. Several neighbors had taken photos of coyotes in their yards and we had seen bobcats in the area. Trouble was very territorial, fighting with any cat who walked into our yard. I worried that Trouble would take on a bobcat twice her size.

Trouble always enjoyed a good cat fight. We had several other cats coming into our yard regularly, including a Scottish Fold, a black cat and a tiger cat. One morning, when she was still an outdoor cat, I looked in the backyard and saw a ball of orange and black fur rolling across the grass. Trouble was fighting with Allie Cat, the orange tabby cat who lived next door. Allie Cat liked to sleep in our flower garden so she also claimed our yard as her territory. This was the beginning of a contentious relationship between the two cats.

Trouble and Allie Cat still fight through the screen in the sunroom. Allie Cat sits outside, taunting our cat. Trouble jumps on the screen with all four paws and her claws get stuck in the thick mesh of the screen. I have to pull her off before she panics about being stuck two feet off the floor.

One spring night, with a bright yellow full moon shining in our open windows, Trouble was very restless and agitated. She paced back and forth in front of the door, howling and looking sad and forlorn.

"You have to stay inside, Trouble," I said, talking loudly over her caterwauling. I tried to pick her up and comfort her, but she dug her front claws into my forearm until I released her. I knew she wanted to go outside, but she needed to stay inside where she was safe.

Professor was already sleeping since he leaves early for his long commute to work. I tiptoed into the bedroom and started getting ready to go to bed.

Suddenly, I heard a loud crash. I ran toward the sound and arrived just in time to see a tail going out the window. Trouble had pushed the screen out of the open window and jumped outside. I looked out the window, and watched the blur of tan, white and black fur streaking across the yard. Trouble was ecstatic. She ran straight for the pine forest behind our house – a dangerous place for a house cat.

"She'll be back in the morning for breakfast," I said, confidently to the empty room.

I woke up earlier than usual the next morning, realizing that the cat was not purring in my ear. I became fully alert as I remembered the events of the night before. I hopped out of bed and ran to the sunroom, expecting to see Trouble's adorable face peering at me through the glass door. Trouble was not in the sunroom. I felt the panic welling up in my chest. I was very attached to this cat and did not want her to come to any harm. I tried calling Professor at work to get some sage advice, but he did not answer the phone.

I assumed the worst must have happened. Trouble's internal meal clock is very reliable. She sits by her bowl at exactly the same time every morning and evening, waiting for her food. If Trouble was late for breakfast, the only logical conclusion was that there must be something very wrong.

Grabbing my helmet and jumping on my bike, I rode all around the neighborhood, calling her name. I'm sure the neighbors thought I was crazy as I rode by calling, "Trouble! Trouble!" I didn't care; I was too worried about my cat.

Next, I talked to the neighbors. I walked up and down the street, knocking on doors, asking neighbors if they had seen her. "No, no, no…" The responses were all the same. No one had seen my cat.

Professor came home from work at 4 p.m. and I accosted him as he walked in the door. "Trouble's gone!" I yelled, almost hysterical by this point. This precocious kitty had quickly moved to the center of my world. The mere thought of going through each day without my little buddy sitting near my desk made my chest constrict with panic and my eyes fill to overflowing. I could not imagine my life without Trouble.

Always methodical, Professor sat down and took out a piece of paper and a pencil. "Okay, let's try to relax a minute and come up with a strategy. I'm sure we'll find her." Professor hugged me, trying to make me feel better. It didn't work.

"No doubt she's sleeping under a bush somewhere, exhausted from prowling all night," Professor continued. "Let's have some tea and write a list." He knows making lists helps to focus my anxious mind.

We made a list and started following it while dividing up the tasks to be more efficient in our search. We even recruited some neighborhood kids to help with the search, bribing them with Professor's homemade chocolate chip cookies. The kids helped me make signs and we posted them around the neighborhood. I berated myself for not having a good photo of the cat. One of the kids drew a picture with crayons – an adorable cat picture but not a true likeness of Trouble.

Professor stayed by the telephone, coordinating the search. He called everyone we could think of – the Humane Society, local veterinarians, animal control, police and fire departments. Each phone call ended the same. "Okay, thanks for checking your records," Professor said, politely, after the party on the other end said they had not seen our cat.

I sat at my computer trying to work, but my mind was unable to focus on anything work-related. Staring at the computer screen, all of my thoughts were consumed by my missing cat. With each passing hour, I could feel the dread creeping into my thoughts. I was terrified that I might never find Trouble.

Finally, I gave up on being productive and decided to continue the search for the cat. I put on pants and boots, walking in the deep woods behind our house, calling, "Trouble, come here, kitty!" I walked slowly, looking carefully for rattlesnakes, alligators and giant banana spiders. Recently, I had seen a large Eastern Diamondback rattlesnake wrapped around the base of the pole of one of our birdhouses. The mockingbird was sitting on the sunroom roof, screeching loudly, to alert everyone a dangerous snake was in the area. I tried not to think of what would happen if Trouble ran into one of these large, venomous snakes.

Finally, at dusk when the mosquitoes were swarming in a cloud around my head, I gave up, and went home. There was no sign of our cat. Tears ran down my face as I worried about what might have happened to her. Falling exhausted into bed, I had a picture of Trouble in my mind – injured and hungry, unable to get home. I didn't sleep well.

I jumped out of bed the next morning, slipped on my yard shoes, and ran out to the sunroom. With every step I was hoping for a miracle. And just like that, there she was. As soon as she saw me, she started meowing softly to let me know she was very hungry. "Hello, my sweet cat!" I said, overjoyed, as I rushed to the door. I scooped her up to squeeze her, trying to convey the enormity of my relief in seeing her adorable face again. She did not like being squeezed and let me know with a squawk. Thankfully, she appeared uninjured. My anxiety dissipated and my fears were replaced with joy.

Now approaching late middle age, Trouble has adjusted to being an indoor cat. She spends her mornings and afternoons soaking up the sun as it shines through the window in the sunroom. Even at the age of 13, she still runs and plays, chasing anything that moves. She jumps on the screen trying to catch chameleons and frogs that are crawling on the screen outside.

Occasionally, one of the small reptiles gets into the sunroom. Recently, Professor was sitting at the computer and Trouble came up next to his chair and grunted. "What's the matter, kitty?" he said, looking down at the cat near his feet. A long tail was sticking out of her mouth. Eating anything other than cat food makes Trouble ill. When she was an outdoor cat, Trouble would deposit the half-digested remains of reptiles on to the living room carpet. With this in mind, Professor yelled, "Drop it!" The cat dropped the small chameleon, which ran quickly across the floor and out into the sunroom. Trouble charged after it, and kept yowling for her prey long after Professor caught it and threw it outside.

Trouble enjoys playing games. Every night after dinner, Trouble squawks until Professor or I play with her. First we play soccer; I roll a ball to her and she bats it with her paw. Next, we play with a shoestring. She runs and jumps on the string just like a kitten. After our play time, I put the shoestring away. Otherwise, she will eat it like a piece of spaghetti.

Trouble has become a well-loved member of our family, at the center of our world. Everything about our lives changed when she adopted us; she prescribed our new routines. Once we learned to understand each other, she was key in helping us to adapt to her needs. This communication was essential when we began traveling with our beloved cat.

6 YELLOWSTONE NATIONAL PARK

As I was sorting through some files in my office, several photos fell on the floor. Trouble watched me with curiosity, walked over to the photos and sniffed them. She swatted the photos with her right paw and then went back to her spot to sit and watch me work.

I picked up the photos and realized they were from one of our first trips to the western part of the United States. One photo showed Mom standing in a parking lot in Yellowstone National Park. A male elk with huge antlers was standing a few yards away. A small child stood next to the elk, while the child's mother stood nearby taking a photo with a camera.

The photo released a flood of memories. Before we had a cat, Professor and I planned several trips so we could tour the West including Yellowstone National Park. I had never been to the West. Professor's stories from a trip with his family, when they drove from Philadelphia, Pennsylvania to Los Angeles, California, intrigued me. I wanted to see the national parks, wide-open spaces and snow-capped mountains that he talked about.

One of Professor's favorite stories involved a special sunrise. Professor recalled waking up at sunrise in the back seat of the family's station wagon while they were driving through New Mexico. His father was driving while his mother and sisters were sleeping.

"I looked out the window and saw the sun rising over the desert. The first rays of the sun cut through the intense darkness of the desert. My father noticed that I was awake. He smiled and talked about the amazing scene playing out in front of us," Professor said dreamily, thinking about the shared moment.

Professor also remembered the first time he saw the Rocky Mountains. The sight of the immense peaks changed his perspective and after that time, he felt drawn to return to the mountains in the West.

We spent one fast-paced summer vacation touring around the West.

Professor planned a trip that took us to several national parks and a number of states – all in the course of two weeks. We invited Mom and Dad to go with us, since they had never traveled out West.

We rented a four-door sedan and spent long hours in the car driving from one destination to the next. I do not enjoy long car rides; they remind me of family trips when I was a kid, squashed in the back seat of the car with my two sisters. However, the enchanting scenery with snow-capped mountains and wide-open spaces held my attention, taking my mind off the discomfort of sitting in the car. This whirlwind tour allowed us a brief visit in each place, giving us the flavor of these western spaces.

Sitting in the car for endless hours with my parents was challenging. I come from a family of tall people so there was very little extra space in the car. Professor was the primary driver. He enjoys driving and playing tour guide so he spent most of the time in the driver's seat. Dad sat in the front passenger seat, alternating between dozing, acting as a passenger seat driver, telling Professor to "Watch out!" and looking for photo opportunities.

I sat in the rear seat behind Professor, looking at the back of his head with what little hair remained on it. I was usually reading or trying to take a nap. Mom was in the back seat next to me, sitting behind Dad who had his seat pushed all the way back to accommodate his 6-foot 3-inch frame. A pile of books and newspapers sat on the seat in-between Mom and me, acting as a barrier.

One particular day was memorable. I still have the photo which captured the unusual events.

"It's going to be hot today with a chance of thunderstorms in the late afternoon," Mom said. She was reading the morning newspaper – out loud; a habit that can be annoying after several hours.

With Dad sitting in the front seat reading directions, interjecting an occasional "Turn here," and Mom reading the newspaper out loud, it was hard to have a quiet moment to hear my own thoughts.

"Oh, we just missed a great shot of the river!" Dad exclaimed during a drive down a dusty country road. Professor had decided to take the scenic route to our hotel. The sun was sitting low on the horizon and the orange light was reflecting off the nearby river. Small mammals were scurrying about collecting their evening meals.

"Okay, we can stop," Professor replied, always patient with Dad's demands for photo opportunities. Professor turned the car around and drove slowly back down the dusty road until Dad yelled "Stop!"

Dad hopped out of the car holding onto his expensive camera. We all looked toward the nearby river to enjoy the scenery and to see what was so special about this spot.

"Stop!" Mom cried, putting her hand over Dad's camera lens.

"What are you doing?" Dad yelled, annoyed at Mom for interfering with his photo of the sunlight on the river.

Mom pointed her finger at the river and we all looked in that direction. A pair of teenagers were floating down the river on a raft. The girl was sunbathing – nude.

Professor was embarrassed and started walking toward the car. Dad pointed his camera, trying to take a photo, but Mom restrained him.

"Okay, I think we have seen enough here," I said, feeling like an intruder. We were on a backcountry road; the only car for miles around. "I'm sure the teenagers didn't expect to have an audience on their trip down the river," I added.

As I turned to get into the car, I noticed a "Dead End" sign next to the road. The sign was at the entrance to a little-used, unpaved road littered with small boulders and deep pot holes. I looked across the wide-open space to the horizon; I couldn't see anything except the outline of the mountains turning purple as the sun set in a glow of orange. I took a photo of the sign and the wide-open space behind it and later hung it on the wall of my office. The "Dead End" sign became symbolic of my job in corporate America and my reasons for quitting the job to become a teacher.

Climbing back into the car, we resumed our positions. Dad was certain we were lost, so he was reading the map. Professor was nodding his head patiently and responding with the occasional, "Okay, Dad." Dad seemed to forget that Professor has a photographic memory. Professor spent hours studying the maps before we left for the trip. By the time we picked up the rental car, he knew exactly where to go, as if he had driven the route many times. We arrived safely at our hotel and immediately went to bed.

We drove to Jackson, Wyoming and spent the next day visiting Grand Teton National Park. As we entered the park, Professor gave us a history lesson, spouting facts that he read on the National Park Service website, nps.gov. "Grand Teton National Park celebrates the sheer majesty of the Rocky Mountain Range. Spanning a distance of 3,000 miles from British Columbia in Canada to southwestern New Mexico, the 'Rockies', as they are commonly called, define the American West. Grand Teton National Park protects 310,000 acres of glacial lakes, pristine rivers and waterfalls, and the towering peaks of the Teton Range. Visitors often gaze open-mouthed at the beautiful skyline presented by the Tetons."

We were in awe at the size of the mountains. "They make the mountains on the East Coast look like hills," I said to Professor, huffing and puffing as we hiked up a trail to a mountain lake. We were not used to the higher elevation.

Professor nodded, deep in reflective thought about the amazing scenery. We hiked to a lake and sat quietly, eating our sandwiches. We vowed to return to Grand Teton National Park on another trip and spend more time exploring the area.

The next day we drove to Yellowstone National Park, which is not too far from Grand Teton National Park. Professor gave us an overview of the park, including information from nps.gov. "Perhaps the most famous park in the world, Yellowstone National Park was likely the first national park when it was established in 1872. The Yellowstone area is essentially a giant volcano where the earth's crust is very thin resulting in a geologic 'hot spot.' The energy from the hot spot powers the more than 300 geysers and thermal structures located throughout the area, the single largest concentration of geothermal features on Earth. The unique geology has resulted in a lush landscape with an abundance of animals."

Driving through the southern end of Yellowstone, we were impressed by the diversity of the environment and creatures living there. "Yellowstone has more large mammals than anywhere in North America outside Alaska. Pristine rivers and lakes crisscross the park and further support both animals and humans," Professor added.

Yellowstone is full of surprises. A wolf ran across the road in front of us and we all got very excited. Our first destination was the famous Yellowstone geyser – Old Faithful. Located in the southwest section of the park, the geyser was named for its frequent and predictable eruptions. Professor gave us a mini-lecture on Old Faithful as we sat on nearby benches waiting for the next eruption.

"The ranger station in the area tracks the time, height and length of an eruption. The data allows the rangers to estimate the time of the next eruption. The time between eruptions ranges from 60 to 110 minutes. The rangers post the estimated time for the next eruption in the buildings around Old Faithful." Professor stopped to take a breath as Old Faithful started to spurt water.

The geyser started shooting steaming water, 90 to 180 feet in the air, close to the predicted time. We said "Ooh!" and "Ahh!" along with the crowd while taking many photos. The Old Faithful Lodge is next to the geyser, so we went inside to tour the museum, get maps from the helpful National Park Service Rangers and have a snack in the cafeteria. Then we were ready to see more. We walked around the Upper Geyser Basin following the path near Old Faithful to see the 150 geysers in the area. Some of the geysers are much larger than Old Faithful, but their eruptions are less predictable. Old Faithful gets the spotlight because of its predictability, making it a real crowd-pleaser.

We left the Old Faithful area, driving through the park and stopping at some of the scenic walkways off the main road. The geysers are impressive, but I was fascinated by the colorful mud pots. The giant, hot, bubbling pools of mud reminded me of oatmeal boiling on the stove – making gurgling sounds while thick pieces of brown mud exploded out of the hole. As much as I wanted to get a closer look, I realized that it's best to heed the signs warning visitors to stay on the walkway. Boiling mud will burn a hole through your skin.

After having our fill of Yellowstone's volcanic features, we decided to drive to our final destination for the day, Lake Yellowstone Hotel. We drove across the park in the late afternoon, fully engaged in the scenery and wildlife surrounding us. We pulled off at one scenic overlook to view the herd of elk in the valley. Looking across the parking lot, I saw a lone male elk with huge antlers standing at the edge of the pavement. Mom was standing between me and the elk – a safe distance from the elk. "Turn around, Mom," I directed. I took a photo of Mom with the elk in the background.

As I put the camera down, I realized I had captured another scene. A woman with a young child walked up to the elk, pushed the child right next to the elk's right front leg and then stepped back to take a photo. "Wow! That lady is brave," Mom said, aghast. We watched in horror, waiting for the elk to react and injure the child or the mother.

"Crazy," Dad muttered, while turning away, not wanting to see what would happen.

There are signs all over Yellowstone warning visitors that wildlife is unpredictable and people should stay a safe distance from all of the animals. Some people choose to ignore the signs. They seem to think they are in a petting zoo where the animals are domesticated and not dangerous. This couldn't be further from the truth. Tourists who don't heed the warnings are often injured by the frightened animals.

"Let's get to our hotel," Professor said, opening the car doors. We quickly climbed into the car to drive to our hotel. We couldn't watch anymore.

Professor drove the car on the main road through the park, while Dad, Mom and I dozed. We were tired and hungry after a full day in the park. Professor followed the map in his mind and turned toward the Lake Yellowstone Hotel. We breathed a collective sigh of relief, ready to sit in a motionless chair and relax.

Suddenly, Professor jammed on the brakes. "Hey!" I cried as my head snapped back and my glasses fell into my lap. Mom picked up the newspaper which she had dropped on the floor.

Looking ahead on the road, we saw a long line of red brake lights.

"Oh, no, an accident!" Dad cried. He had been complaining that it was past his dinner time. "We'll miss dinner and go to bed hungry," he moaned.

I was hungry too; my stomach growling at the mention of dinner.

Professor is always optimistic. "I don't think it's an accident," he chimed in, squinting and leaning forward to try to see what was happening ahead of our car.

"Most likely some type of animal blocking the road," Mom added, while reading the Park's newspaper. "They call it an animal jam. This is the term used by Park Rangers to describe the traffic jams created when people stop to watch wildlife."

We all stared at the long line of cars ahead of us as Professor slowed our car to a stop. We couldn't see anything besides the cars. We sat quietly for a few minutes, each of us thinking about the implications of being stuck in traffic.

Without warning, our car was surrounded by bison. Everywhere we looked, the huge animals were moving slowly around the cars and across the road.

"It is an animal jam!" I shouted, gleefully. Although the Yellowstone brochures were full of pictures of bison, we had not seen any of the large animals. This was our first time seeing a bison, and now we were surrounded by a whole herd.

"Bison are an integral part of our country's history," Professor explained. "In the 19th century, the bison were hunted to near extinction. The herd in Yellowstone is significant since it has been there since the park was founded and was a fundamental part of the preservation of the species. Yellowstone now has an estimated 4,500 bison in the park."

A large male bison stopped right next to our car. Everyone in the car reacted at once. Mom was yelling, "Get your camera!" while Dad was fumbling with his large camera bag, trying to get the equipment out. He started to open the car door to get out and create some room for his camera.

"No, Dad, no!" I screamed, jumping out of my seat to grab his shoulder. The huge bison was standing right next to the passenger side mirror. Stepping out of the car would put Dad in mortal danger.

Dad finally got his camera out of the case and snapped a photo. The bison was peering in through the car window, looking intently at us, as we stared back at him.

We all went silent, realizing the power of a 2,000-pound animal. "Hello nice bison," I whispered, hoping in some strange way it might keep the bison calm instead of ramming his impressive horns into our rental car. After a series of grunts, the bison stepped away from the car, merging into the stream of bison crossing the road in front of us.

We sat in traffic for some time after the herd moved on, but we didn't mind. Seeing the bison herd up close was awe-inspiring.

We arrived at the Lake Yellowstone Hotel in the early evening. After a quick shower, we headed to the restaurant. We were famished after our adventurous day in the park. Built in 1891, the Lake Yellowstone Hotel is the oldest hotel in the park and a National Historic Landmark. The hotel has the charm of that era even though it has recently been renovated, adding internet access and other amenities. Walking into the sunroom off the hotel lobby, we stopped to admire the interior of the hotel. The hotel's simple elegance creates a relaxing atmosphere.

We enjoyed western fare at the restaurant, eating bison and elk burgers with potatoes and crisp green salads. After dinner, we strolled into the sunroom. Surrounded by windows, the sunroom allows an unobstructed view of Lake Yellowstone. The summer sun was setting and the lake was alive with movement from insects, fish and wildlife coming to the lake for an evening meal or drink.

"Awesome! It's so gorgeous and relaxing," I said, looking around the bright, inviting room.

"Neat," Dad responded, still sluggish from eating a large meal.

"Can we please sit down?" Mom, always impatient, was scanning the room for unoccupied chairs.

Professor started to offer a history of the hotel, but his voice was drowned out by the sound of the piano. The piano player in the center of the room was accompanied by string instruments, playing a rousing rendition of a classic rock song. Glancing around the room, I saw many families sitting together playing board games, enjoying snacks and drinks, and tapping their feet to the beat of the music. I took a deep breath and released the stress of travelling. There was no place that I would rather be at this moment.

We found a seat on the comfortable furniture and enjoyed the music, scenery and the soothing vibe. Watching the light and colors on the lake change as the sun set, we relaxed. Eventually we were all nodding off – tired from a long day of touring the park and relaxed from the music and the comfortable furniture. I looked over at Dad, already asleep with his chin resting on his chest. He can sleep anywhere.

"Time for bed, everyone," Mom said, rousing herself from a half-asleep stupor. She poked Dad in the arm, waking him up with a start.

Professor and I stood up, ready to have some time to ourselves. "Good night, see you in the morning," we said in unison, waving to my parents as we walked through the lobby toward our room. Mom and Dad were busy squabbling about what time they would wake up for breakfast.

Professor and I fell into bed in the sparsely decorated room. At that time, there were no electronic devices in the room – no television, no radio and no telephone. We felt peaceful and content, appreciating the darkness and total silence as an opportunity for much needed rest.

Suddenly, I heard a loud howling noise – then another and another – until there was a chorus of howling. I bolted upright in bed, bumping Professor with my elbow at the same time. "Ugh," he groaned in his sleep.

I poked him again. "What's that noise?" I asked, turning on the light. It was pitch black in the room due to the lack of light from outside – great for sleeping, but creepy when there are strange noises.

"Wolves," Professor replied, turning over to go back to sleep. "Go back to bed."

I am a light sleeper, hearing every noise during the night and waking up in a panic when I don't recognize the noise. I lay awake imagining the group of wolves standing on a mountainside, howling together, communicating with the members of their pack. I calmly reminded myself that this was one of the reasons why we came to Yellowstone and soon fell asleep with this picture in my mind.

Much too soon, we finished this first tour of the West and returned to our home and jobs. After a couple of weeks, Professor and I were back into our regular routine. However, we were not the same people; we were altered by the experience. We could not get the images of the West out of our minds. We developed our film and poured over the hundreds of photos, reminiscing about our favorite places and planning future trips. We selected some of our favorite photos and had them enlarged to poster size. The photos became a part of our home and offices, continually reminding us of our connection to these Western places.

7 PET SITTER PROBLEMS

Professor and I continued to take trips out West at every opportunity. We hadn't adopted Trouble quite yet, so we were free to travel to different places. We spent all of our summer vacations exploring different towns in the West, always renting an apartment so we could cook our own food and stay close to mountain hiking trails. We talked about buying a condo in a Western town, but we could not afford it on our teachers' salaries.

A later trip to Yellowstone with my sister Kathy, her husband, and my niece and nephew, was a pivotal point in our planning. We agreed to meet by Old Faithful and we spotted my niece and nephew as they ran to greet us with big hugs. They had already signed up for the Junior Ranger program and talked non-stop about all of the things they wanted to do and see. Their enthusiasm was refreshing; I saw too many kids staring at their cell phones while grumbling about having "no connection." Those kids were missing out on the Yellowstone experience.

We spent a couple of days visiting and touring different areas of the park. My niece and nephew continued to be excited about everything they experienced, whether it was a herd of bison or a chipmunk. Their joy for discovering things in Yellowstone was contagious and we found ourselves seeing familiar sights from a new perspective.

We stayed at the Lake Yellowstone Hotel again, reminiscing about the first time we visited the hotel with Mom and Dad. In the evenings, we sat listening to the live piano music in the conservatory. My niece bravely took a five-dollar bill up to the piano player and requested her favorite tune – quite a feat for a six-year-old.

Kathy and her family had flown into Bozeman, Montana which is two hours from Yellowstone. We all drove back to Bozeman where we stayed for a few days to rest before traveling home. This was our first trip to Bozeman and we did not know a lot about the area. Professor and I took some time to walk around Bozeman and immediately felt a strong attachment to the place. It felt very familiar – a vibrant Main Street like the one we frequented when we lived in Pennsylvania, hiking trails on the edge of town, similar to other towns out West and a network of paved multi-use paths. Bozeman appeared to have all of our favorite things.

Professor and I had discussed spending time out West when we retired from our jobs. However, we hadn't been able to find affordable real estate in any of our desired destinations. Professor decided we should look at condos in Bozeman so we visited several real estate offices, but we left with our usual disappointment. The prices were too high for our budget.

Several years later, we were still thinking about buying a small condo so we would have a permanent place to stay. Trouble was now an integral part of our family and we wanted to have our own place so we did not have to worry about taking her to hotels.

The Great Recession altered our plans. The real estate market had crashed and prices had become affordable. We scrimped and saved, looking for every opportunity to put extra money in the bank. Professor created a budget and we reduced our expenses.

Professor spent several hours each week looking online for real estate in Bozeman that fit in our budget. "We need to go back to Bozeman to look at condos," he said one afternoon, while staring at a long list of properties for sale. "It's a buyer's market."

"Go back to Bozeman? I liked Bozeman, but we couldn't afford any of the places that were for sale. I think we should go somewhere else – a place where we might have a chance to find something affordable," I replied. I was tired of getting excited about having a place in a mountain town and then being disappointed by high prices.

"We should take a trip to Bozeman. I just have a feeling," he said adamantly. Professor always has "a feeling" when he is trying to convince me to see things from his viewpoint.

I nodded my head, only half listening. We had discussed this idea many times, in many different places. Owning property in a mountain town sounded ideal, but it was not feasible with our modest income.

Eventually Professor won the argument and we planned a trip to Bozeman. Once we decided we were going to Bozeman for two weeks, we had to find someone to take care of Trouble, who was now a house cat. We decided to hire a pet sitter so Trouble could stay in her own home. Our friend recommended a pet sitter who watched her dogs every week. We asked the pet sitter to come for an interview with Professor, me and Trouble.

The pet sitter arrived on schedule – a positive start in my time-oriented mind. Professor opened the door and she strolled in, glancing at us briefly while saying, "Where's the cat?"

She had barely spoken the words when Trouble came running across the room, flung her body at the woman's feet and started rolling around. This behavior usually means, "Pet me, my friend!"

I was shocked. Trouble likes people and always runs near the door when she hears the doorbell. However, as a former stray cat, she is cautious around strangers, making sure the person is friendly and nice before she commits herself to a relationship.

This woman must be something special – like Dr. Doolittle, I thought. Then I looked at her more closely. The woman was short with a wide girth as she enjoyed eating regularly at all of her stops. She expected clients to leave food for her in the refrigerator. Her short, wavy, gray hair was untamed and out of control. She was wearing a loose floral dress which didn't fit well and smelled like body odor. I wrinkled my nose before realizing I was being rude. Looking at the floor to avoid showing my distaste for the smell, I noticed that each of her fingers had several rings on them.

I walked over to introduce myself, but she ignored me. She was busy playing with Trouble, who apparently adored this woman. I could tell from Trouble's body language that she was relaxed and happy, enjoying attention from her new friend. The woman finally remembered that there were humans in the room and looked up at Professor and me. "Oh, I'm Lucy." We introduced ourselves and sat down at the dining room table so we could get to know one another.

"Would you like a cup of tea?" Professor asked Lucy. He welcomes all guests into our home this way since he was raised on the idea of Southern hospitality.

"Yes, and a snack, if you have one," Lucy replied. I raised my eyebrows in surprise, but Professor is an expert baker, having worked in a bakery when he was in high school. He enjoys sharing his baked goods so he put a homemade muffin on a plate. Lucy ate the muffin with great gusto while also petting Trouble, who was now sitting on Lucy's feet. Trouble ate the crumbs that fell on the floor.

We interviewed Lucy for an hour, asking lots of questions about how she would care for Trouble while we were traveling. She was charming in an eclectic sort of way and convinced us that she had lots of experience as a pet sitter and cat lover. Lucy also mentioned that her husband hated cats. This was of little concern until she said that her husband was the backup pet sitter if anything happened to her. She appeared to be in good health, so we dismissed the idea.

We decided to hire Lucy because she was the best candidate, our friend assured us that she was an excellent pet sitter and Trouble adored her. I spent several days organizing everything for the pet sitter, including three pages of instructions with all of the details about our cat's habits – food, water, medicine, litter box, toys and more. I printed the instructions and left them on the kitchen counter along with Trouble's toys and the pet sitter's check.

I also left some of Professor's homemade baked treats for Lucy in the refrigerator.

Just thinking about leaving Trouble was painful. Since she became a house cat, we had not been separated for more than a few hours at a time. The idea of leaving her with a stranger for a few weeks was heart-wrenching. Since I often worked at home, we spent entire days together. She was my little buddy, following me around, rubbing my legs, talking to me and napping on the nearest soft piece of furniture. I worried constantly that Trouble would be stressed if the pet sitter did not do things the way she liked them. Eventually, I decided to trust the pet sitter based on her years of experience and references.

When it was time for us to leave for Bozeman, Trouble sat by the front door watching Professor as he took the luggage out to the car. I picked her up, giving her a hug and a kiss on the head. "I will miss you, sweet kitty," I said, not wanting to let her go. She tolerated my affections for a few minutes and then squirmed until I put her down. As she disappeared into the other room to find her favorite sunny spot, I forced myself to leave the house. I hoped the pet sitter would do a good job.

On our first day in Bozeman, Professor and I met our realtor in her office. Coming from the East coast where dress codes are more formal, I was surprised to see her wearing a plaid shirt, faded jeans and cowboy boots. We climbed into her pickup truck and began our hunt for affordable real estate. The realtor gave us an overview of the real estate market. "There are only five properties in your price range," she explained.

Professor, sitting in the front seat, nodded his head optimistically. I felt depressed. How could we find a place in our modest price range with only five properties to choose from?

The choice was easy. The first property was out of our price range and a dump that smelled like engine oil. "It's a great downtown location," our realtor said, trying to sound positive while holding her nose.

"Right; next place," I responded, walking quickly out the door because I could barely breathe in the stinky house.

The next property was new construction and in our price range. It was very small, but I liked that everything was brand new, especially the kitchen, since Professor and I enjoy cooking and baking. I found myself being drawn to the place, nodding enthusiastically as the realtor rattled off the benefits of the location. Then I walked out onto the balcony; it had a lovely view of the parking lot. I imagined noisy neighbors coming and going at all hours of the night while I tossed and turned in my bed, unable to sleep because of the noise.

"Everything here is brand new. I really like the kitchen!" Professor exclaimed while opening the oven so he could imagine it filled with his baked goods. He stood in the middle of the kitchen with a faraway look and I knew he was thinking about cooking a meal for a group of people – something he really enjoys.

"Too loud," I complained as I walked back into the living room. The realtor responded with a long list of benefits of buying the condo, but I ignored her. I need my sleep; no one wants to be around me when I haven't had my sleep.

The next property was in a neighborhood on the edge of town. We walked upstairs to a second-floor condo and waited as the realtor unlocked the door. Suddenly, the door swung open by itself and the realtor dropped her key on the ground. A woman in a loose bathrobe stuck her head out the door and shouted, "What are you doing?"

The realtor looked shocked and then recovered her professional demeanor. "I'm sorry; I was told the property was vacant," the realtor said evenly, as if this happens all of the time.

"This is my home!" the woman yelled while slamming the door in our faces. I looked down at my list and crossed off that address.

The next property was not in a great location and was listed as "sale pending." We decided not to waste our time.

Finally, we went to the last property on our list – a condo in an older neighborhood. The condo was small, but the bedrooms were on the second floor, making it seem like it had more space. The property had a small backyard with a fence – something that appealed to us right away. We like to look at trees, flowers and birds. The condo had been a rental property and was clearly a fixer-upper with holes in the walls, damaged floors and stains on the kitchen ceiling from the upstairs bathroom. However, Professor and I liked the property and he was excited about being able to do some home improvement projects.

While eating dinner that evening, we debated the advantages and disadvantages of buying a condo in Bozeman. We narrowed down the choices to the new construction and the fixer-upper, but my aversion to loud noises won the argument. Professor called the realtor and made a low bid offer on the fixer-upper and the offer was accepted. The seller was tired of managing renters and didn't want to put any more money into the property. We were now the proud owners of a small, beat-up condo in Bozeman, Montana.

While we were shopping for real estate in Bozeman, I worried about Trouble and whether the new pet sitter was taking good care of her. "Do you think the cat is okay?" I asked Professor, at least 10 times a day.

"Yes, she's fine," he replied. He doesn't worry about things the way that I do and had confidence in Lucy's experience.

In my instructions, I asked Lucy to call us every day to let us know how Trouble was doing. I checked my messages several times a day – no calls. "Have you checked your messages? Are there any messages from Lucy?" I persisted.

"I checked and there are no messages," Professor replied.

Since we hadn't heard from Lucy, I called her. She didn't have a cell phone, so I called her home phone number. No one answered the phone and I heard the click of an old-fashioned answering machine.

"Hi Lucy, I'm just calling to check on Trouble. I wanted to see how she's doing," I said, keeping my message brief, and trying to sound cheerful. Lucy didn't call me back. I did my best to be patient, but after 24 hours, I called again and left another message on the answering machine.

Professor and I were exploring some of Bozeman's hiking trails, talking excitedly about our plans for the condo. He had already been studying the maps and targeting areas that he wanted to explore. He was telling me about his plans when his cell phone rang. "Hi Lucy," Professor said cheerfully. I heard Lucy talking loudly and quickly while Professor's eyebrows closed together in a scowl.

"What's wrong?" I asked, feeling my chest tighten with panic. "Is there something wrong with our cat?" Professor raised his hand, gesturing for me to be silent so he could hear what Lucy was saying.

I paced back and forth while Professor listened to Lucy and then gave her some brief instructions. Finally, he ended the call and explained the situation to me. Lucy was frantic because Trouble had eaten the piece of string that I left for her to use during playtime with the cat. Trouble enjoys chasing string and it's a great way to get her running around. However, I always keep the string in a plastic bag because Trouble likes to eat the string – sucking it up like a piece of spaghetti.

Lucy had forgotten to put the string back in the bag and Trouble had jumped up on the counter and eaten the string. This was serious; the string could kill Trouble if it got stuck in her intestines. Lucy promised to watch Trouble carefully over the next couple of days to see if she had any problems. I worried and fretted, picturing my cat in pain or worse. Also, I no longer trusted Lucy to make good decisions about Trouble's care. Leaving string out on the counter for a cat who would swallow it was an unforgiveable mistake.

Lucy called a couple of days later to say that the cat seemed okay, but she was avoiding her litter box. Although Trouble routinely avoided her box when she was feeling anxious, the pet sitter said Trouble had messed in the middle of the living room. This had never happened before. I was concerned that this was a sign of a serious medical problem and I panicked. We changed our itinerary and I flew home the next day.

Arriving home, I was greeted by a very unhappy cat. As I fumbled with the keys in the locks, I heard Trouble on the other side of the door, yowling loudly – she was very agitated. I opened the door and the cat yowled louder. Tossing my luggage on the floor, I picked Trouble up and hugged her, reassuring her it would be "okay." However, I was really worried about the string in her intestines, thinking I had better call the veterinarian.

On top of my original instructions on the counter, I found a scribbled note from Lucy saying, "I tried to clean up as best as I could." Lying next to the instructions was the empty plastic bag which originally kept the string out of Trouble's reach. I shook my head in frustration as I walked around the house for an inspection so I could see how well the pet sitter had cared for my cat.

I walked over to Trouble's food and water bowls. Eating is one of her favorite things and she gets very anxious if her food and water are not the way she likes them. The first thing I noticed was the open can of cat food, sitting on the counter. Trouble eats wet food which has to be refrigerated. The food had not spoiled, but I wondered if Lucy was leaving the food out every day and then feeding it to the cat. I opened the trash can to throw out the food and saw a pile of waste from her litter box. My instructions specified putting the litter box waste in the garbage can in the garage. The kitchen trash can was right next to the cat's bowl. Trouble would be upset if she had to eat while smelling the waste from her box.

Looking at the water bowl, I could see a thick layer of cat fur floating on top of the water. It's important for a cat to drink water regularly, to avoid urinary tract infections. My instructions had been very specific; Trouble will only drink water if the water is very clean and the bowl is filled to the brim. The pet sitter was supposed to put fresh water in the dish every day. Clearly, the water had not been refreshed for a number of days.

I found myself getting annoyed but tried to calm down. The pet sitter had not followed all of my instructions, but I could see from the dirty food bowl that Trouble was being fed, hopefully on a regular schedule. Trouble was still following me around, yowling loudly, to let me know how upset she was at being left alone.

Next, I checked the litter boxes. I was dismayed. The first litter box was filled to the brim with cat waste. My instructions on cleaning the litter box had been very clear. Trouble is a fastidious cat; she will not use the litter box unless it is very clean. I could see from the mess on the nearby rug that Trouble was avoiding her box because it was dirty.

I didn't see any sign that Trouble had passed or disgorged the string so I was still very worried. Trouble was still yowling, so I worked on making her more comfortable. I gave her some fresh food, and put clean water in her bowl. She started purring – a sure sign she was feeling more relaxed. I cleaned up the messes and put down fresh litter boxes. After eating some food, Trouble settled down and appeared to be content and drowsy.

As I sat on the couch petting the sleeping cat next to me, I felt very angry. We paid Lucy 30 dollars per day to take care of the basic necessities for our cat, including cleaning the litter box and refreshing the water. Instead, Lucy had ignored my instructions and left a mess. She had put Trouble's life at risk by allowing her to eat a long piece of string. As a result of the pet sitter's mistakes, I had to spend several hundred dollars to change my plane ticket to come home for a possible medical emergency.

The cat turned in her sleep, moving closer to my leg. She is adorable and snuggly when she's sleeping. She always has her back leaning up against something, a habit which helps her to feel more secure. When it's cold, she sleeps curled into a perfect donut shape with her tail over her eyes as if she is trying to keep the light out. I stroked her head. "Poor little kitty," I said, feeling guilty for not taking good care of my cat.

I called Professor to update him on the situation. I was angry and spoke quickly, giving him all of the details and making accusations about the pet sitter. He listened in his always patient manner and then calmly said, "We won't hire her again."

The next morning, I found a piece of half-digested string on the carpet. Cleaning up cat barf is not usually a joyful task, but this time I laughed in relief and praised the cat heartily. Trouble had eliminated my worries about the string in her digestive tract.

We found out later that Lucy had been in the hospital during our trip to Bozeman, so her husband, who hated cats, was taking care of Trouble. We sent Lucy a card and felt sorry for her illness. Still, this was not an excuse for the many mistakes which put our cat's health at risk and we vowed never to hire this pet sitter again.

Trouble had recovered from her ordeal by the time Professor returned home. We were now homeowners in Bozeman, Montana. We would need to hire a new pet sitter or the cat would have to travel with us.

8 TRAINING OUR CAT TO TRAVEL

Trouble is usually quiet in the morning until we wake up. Once we wake up, she figures it's okay to be rambunctious – jumping on the bed, licking my arm and purring in my ear. She makes it clear that it's time for her breakfast.

This morning was different. At 4 a.m., Trouble jumped on the bed next to Professor's head and started howling plaintively. Professor woke up and instinctively knew that Trouble needed him to clean up a mess. He went into the kitchen and saw that the cat had barfed up a hairball next to her food bowl. Trouble does not like a mess near her food bowl or litter box.

Professor cleaned up the mess and went back to bed, but the cat was ready to play. As he tried to go back to sleep, she started bouncing around on the bed, purring in his ear, climbing on his stomach and swatting at a fruit fly buzzing around the bedroom. Professor finally got up at 5 a.m.

"Why are you up so early?" I mumbled, half asleep.

"The cat woke me up so I'm going to work early. Don't worry, just go back to sleep," he said as he walked out of the bedroom.

Trouble crawled under the covers on his side of the bed, purring contentedly until we both fell asleep.

This morning's episode reminded me of our struggle to train Trouble. It took lots of patience and expert advice.

Some of the advice came from books by Dr. Temple Grandin. In the chapter on cats in *Animals Make Us Human*, Dr. Grandin grabbed my attention when she wrote, "Dogs serve people, but people serve cats." This made perfect sense. Recently, I had started calling our cat "Queen Trouble" because she ruled our household. My daily schedule was often organized around this demanding creature. While most cats slept all day, Trouble demanded constant attention: petting, feeding and snuggling. She seemed to be training me to do things the way she liked them instead of me training her to be a good pet.

Dr. Grandin explains that cats are still more wild. Cats have been domesticated for a short period of time relative to dogs and other domestic animals. These statements lay the groundwork for training a cat.

With time and patience, Trouble became a well-behaved house cat. Now we were planning our first summer trip to Bozeman and had to figure out how we would train her to travel in the car and stay in hotels.

First, we had to figure out how the cat would ride in the car. We considered putting Trouble in the small pet carrier that we used for visits to the veterinarian, but there is no room for a litter box in the small carrier. Also, she is an active cat, running and jumping during the day and night. She would be too cooped up in a small carrier.

Professor, always full of bright ideas, said, "We should put the cat on a leash. Then we can take her for walks when we are at rest stops. That way, we don't have to worry about the litter box."

"Well, I guess it's worth a try," I replied, thoughtfully. I imagined us walking the cat around a grassy area at a rest stop. She would sniff the grass, swat at the bees, do her business and then we would get back in the car and continue our travels. I bought a cute little animal print harness designed for a small dog and a bright pink leash. I figured the cat could look stylish while she was traveling.

I put the harness in front of Trouble. She looked curiously at the bright colors and sniffed it. She sat patiently as I put the harness on her, securing the straps around her legs and belly. I clipped the leash on in the sunroom for our first "walk." The cat didn't move.

"Okay, Trouble, it's time to walk," I said, pulling gently on the harness, giving her some encouragement. She looked adorable in the animal print harness. She tried to take a step, but the harness restricted her movement – she couldn't walk. The sight was so pathetic that I immediately took the harness off and put it in the donation pile for a local non-profit organization.

"What's your next brilliant idea?" I demanded, glaring at Professor and feeling frustrated. Mostly, I was angry at myself for believing that I could just put a leash on a cat and expect her to walk.

Professor didn't respond. He scowled – a look that means he is thinking deeply and also probably annoyed with me for blaming him for the leash fiasco. Still, he doesn't let anger disturb his creative process and he continued to generate new ideas.

"What if we leave her a space in the back seat with her fuzzy bed?" Professor suggested. "That way, she could nap in her bed and be free to roam around, not feeling cooped up. We could put the litter box at the other end of the seat so she could use it whenever she needed it."

I considered this idea. On a recent trip, we saw a cat sitting on a towel on the console in the front seat of a car. The people were packing the car and the cat was patiently waiting to leave. We have seen other cats sleeping in the sun on the shelf behind the back seat of a sedan. It appeared that some cats settle right down in the car, sleeping peacefully until it's time to get out of the car.

"No, I don't feel comfortable leaving the cat loose in the car," I replied. "She might jump out when we opened the door. If she was scared, she would run away and we would never find her." I imagined Trouble as a stray cat in a rest stop, begging travelers for food and hiding from dogs allowed to run without a leash. I couldn't imagine taking this kind of risk.

We were running out of time and ideas. Then Professor discovered a pet carrier which stretches across the back seat of a car. The carrier is made of mesh, so air can flow through it. Each end has a zipper which can be opened easily and then secured. It has room for the pet to move around with space for a bed and small toys. The carrier is secured with the seatbelt so if the car stops quickly or is in an accident, the pet stays safe. It's light and easy-to-carry, so the pet can go into the carrier in the house or hotel room and be carried safely to the car.

Next, we had to figure out where to stay. Many hotels do not allow pets. The hotels that do accept pets require the owners and their pets to stay in a designated "pet room" and pay a "pet fee." Pet fees can range from 25 dollars to 150 dollars. In addition, hotels have a limited number of pet rooms and these rooms get booked quickly during peak travel seasons. We discovered later that the "pet rooms" are often the least desirable rooms in the hotel.

Professor did some research and made reservations at hotels that accepted pets. Then we focused on training the cat to ride in the car. I continued reading *Animals Make Us Human*. "Kittens and cats should be trained to feel that a cat carrier is a safe place. Food treats can be fed in the carrier and your cat should be gradually taught to tolerate being locked in the carrier for a longer and longer time."

That sounds easy, I thought as I read the book. Trouble will eat just about anything so using treats to motivate her behavior seemed easy.

We put the carrier in the family room so Trouble would have to walk by it to get to her favorite sunny window. I put towels and pillow cases from one of her napping spots inside the carrier and put treats from one end to the other. Trouble smelled the treats and walked through the carrier, gobbling up each treat. Soon the carrier became part of the room.

"This training is easy," I remarked to Professor after Trouble ran through the carrier while we were watching a movie.

Professor nodded thoughtfully. He wasn't convinced.

Once the cat was comfortable with the carrier, it was time to take her for a ride in the car. Up to this point, our experience with the cat in the car had involved trips to the vet. This was always traumatic because Trouble seemed to know we were going to the vet. She would hide and I would spend half-an-hour crawling around the house looking for her. As soon as I got close to her hiding place, she would run to a new spot. After chasing the cat and trying to get her into the small carrier while she splayed all four legs, I was exhausted. Dr. Grandin would be horrified at the scene.

Thinking about the trips to the vet, I continued reading *Animals Make Us Human*. Dr. Grandin explained that cats have high levels of anxiety. They resist change and rarely adapt quickly to new circumstances. This sounded familiar as I have similar levels of anxiety. I tried to view traveling from my cat's perspective.

Great! I thought as I took notes on this section. *We're planning to take a cat away from her favorite sunny spots in her house in Florida to drive her across the country to our condo in Montana. For an animal who does not adapt well to new circumstances, we're asking an awful lot.*

After agonizing over our travel plans and considering the alternatives, I decided it was still the right course of action. Trouble is a smart cat; she learns quickly and remembers what she has learned. She even invents new games and trains me to play them during our evening romps. She is most content when she is with her family. I believed she would be happier traveling with us than being left at home with a pet sitter who did not pay close attention to her needs.

It was time to train the cat to ride in the car. Early one Saturday morning, Professor put the carrier in the car while I tried to catch Trouble. She sensed the change in routine when Professor took the carrier out of the house. I believe she also sensed my anxiety as I started thinking about our plans.

"I'm ready; bring the cat," Professor yelled from the garage. I looked down at my feet where the cat had been sitting moments ago. She had disappeared. I walked all around the house looking in her usual napping spots and couldn't find her.

"I can't find the cat," I shouted back to Professor. I crawled around the house and found the cat underneath our king size bed where I couldn't reach her. She looked anxious as she crouched low under the bed, ready to dash to the next hiding spot. I felt terrible about scaring her into hiding.

I went into the garage to discuss the situation with Professor. "She's hiding under the bed and I can't reach her. I don't want her to associate her first trip in the car with being scared and anxious. Cats can develop a permanent negative association with a person, object or event which can be difficult to overcome. I don't want to take that risk. Our inaugural car trip will have to wait."

I talked rapidly, feeling anxious about training the cat and worried that we would not get the cat trained in time for our May departure. Professor shrugged his shoulders and accepted the situation as he usually does when it appears the odds are against us.

The following week, we were able to easily get the cat into the carrier. We drove around the neighborhood while the cat crouched in a tight ball in the corner of the carrier, yowling loudly. Professor and I couldn't talk because of the noise. I started having visions of driving across the country for 10 days with the cat yowling nonstop. How would we endure this?

I continued reading Dr. Grandin's advice. In Chapter 2 of *Animals in Translation*, Dr. Grandin discusses "How Animals Perceive the World." She writes, "In order to solve a behavioral problem with an animal, you have to go where the animal goes and do what the animal does." Dr. Grandin describes how she often gets down on her hands and knees to follow the tracks of livestock. This allows her to see things from the animals' perspective so she can identify the source of a behavioral problem.

With this in mind, I crawled into the pet carrier and looked around carefully, noticing all of the details. The fabric is black and scratchy with wire covered in fabric that forms the tunnel shape. *Looks dark and uncomfortable,* I thought. The fabric also has a plastic odor, which is probably a lot more powerful in my cat's sensitive nose. The top of the carrier is mesh, allowing light and fresh air to come in, but it also allows the cat to dig her claws into it.

Professor and I discussed my findings during dinner. We decided that Trouble, who can always find the softest blanket in the house, needed some cushioning. Professor designed some padding to go under the carrier using old blankets and thick pads with plastic on the back. We took a soft blanket and put it at the end of the carrier where Trouble was sitting during the first car trip.

We asked our veterinarian for ideas. "Give her something to hide under," he said, brows furrowed. "You know they have coyotes out there, right?" he added with concern. He also gave us some medicine to help Trouble relax since we still did not know how she would behave on the long trip. He said our cat was, "Very healthy" and "Fit for travel."

Following the doctor's advice, we put a well-worn sheet in the carrier. I washed the sheet so it smelled clean and fresh. Our meticulous cat is very particular about cleanliness.

We took our next test drive the following weekend. This time I tried to remain calm. I put Trouble out in the sunroom and closed the door right before we were ready to leave. She was suspicious, but there are no hiding places in the sunroom. I picked her up and could tell from her heartbeat that she was relaxed. I was able to get her into the pet carrier with only a few scratches to show for my efforts.

Professor drove the car a couple of miles to the coffee shop. Trouble was sitting in the far corner of the carrier on top of the blanket, yowling loudly. Professor pulled the car up to the coffee shop drive-thru ordering area and started talking into the speaker. It sounded something like this: "Tall Americano with an extra shot," then "Yowl, yowl, yowl!" This was followed by "Steamed milk with vanilla syrup," and "Yowl, yowl, yowl!"

By the time we drove to the pickup window, our nerves were frazzled and we had only been in the car for 20 minutes. As the barista reached out the window to hand us our drinks, she looked toward the source of the noise. "Is that a cat?" she asked loudly.

"Yes," we replied, shouting so we could be heard over the sound of our cat's yowling. We drove straight home and mulled over the experience while sipping our drinks. The cat ignored us for several hours.

We kept taking Trouble on short test drives, each time taking notes on her behavior. Trouble started to feel more comfortable, getting used to the vibrations of the car and taking short steps. She would yowl for a few minutes and then settle down.

Eventually, Trouble found her "car legs." She started walking back and forth in the carrier, sniffing everything and climbing on the black mesh.

"No, kitty," I said, gently when she dug her claws into the mesh. I felt guilty reprimanding her since we were already asking a lot by driving her around in the car. Her claws got stuck in the mesh, requiring us to stop the car, get out and unhook them. She realized that clawing the mesh meant the car would stop and so she continued to do it.

Mom solved this problem. "Put a sheet over the top of the carrier," she advised. Mom has lots of experience capturing feral cats and taking them to get neutered. She noticed that the cats relaxed when she covered the cage with a sheet. We covered Trouble's pet carrier with a sheet, leaving a space open in front for air flow.

We continued to repeat the practice trips, making them a little longer each time. Soon Trouble started adjusting to the routine. When I picked her up to put her in the carrier, her heart was no longer pounding – just beating at a steady pace. She would yowl loudly for the first 15 minutes and then settle down. I gave her regular treats for good behavior.

We decided to give some of the medicine from the veterinarian to Trouble, to see how it affected her. The veterinarian had demonstrated the process with a cat who lives in their office after being abandoned on the doorstep, making it look easy. I split the pill in half and put it inside a cat treat to disguise the medicine.

Trouble ate the treat greedily – chewing it and swallowing it. I waited expectantly to make sure she swallowed the medicine and then went back to washing dishes while she digested the medicine. As I walked away, I heard the ping of something hard hitting her metal bowl. Trouble had eaten the cat treat and spit out the pill.

"How did she do that?" I asked Professor, continually amazed at how fast our cat learns.

"She's a smart cat," he replied, shaking his head in disbelief.

We were confident that we were more intelligent than our cat and that it was only a matter of finding the right way to give her the medicine. We tried crushing the medicine into tuna oil, using a pill shooter and putting the medicine in her regular cat food. Nothing worked; the cat outsmarted us every time.

Eventually, we gave up on the medicine. We would have to find other ways to keep our cat relaxed on our drive across the country.

After months of planning, training, organizing and packing, it was time to drive to Montana. By this time, the cat had learned to ride comfortably in the car and trained us to meet her needs in the process. My anxiety increased as we got closer to the departure date. I worried about traveling across the country and I worried about my cat.

9 LEAVING JACKSONVILLE

It was one week before our departure for Montana. I sat at the dining room table drinking my coffee – strong and black. Trouble was lying on the carpet next to my feet, perfectly positioned to soak up the slice of spring sunshine coming through the window. Papers were spread across the table – packing lists, task lists, lists for the house sitter and more. I looked through each one, checking to see if items on the list had been completed. I hoped that by the time we left for Montana, everything would be packed in the car and the house would be closed up for the summer.

This was our sixth year of traveling to Bozeman. We learned from mistakes that we made during our earlier trips across the country and there were notes written all over the lists to remind me to do some things differently. The lists included notes about Trouble; our cat is always training us to be better pet owners.

My lists were particularly important for making sure the cat was ready to travel. When driving across the country, it becomes more difficult to find stores which sell her preferred brands of food and litter. Trouble had her own bin full of supplies so that we wouldn't run out of her favorite things. The bin was jammed with cans of her favorite food, her bed, medicines, toys and treats. Next to the bin was the cat's travel bag with basic supplies so I could easily clean the cat's litter box in the car and give her treats to keep her pacified.

The cat's pet carrier sat in the corner of the room. I put treats in the pet carrier daily and the cat walked through it regularly, getting used to the space and remembering the travel routine. As I continued reviewing my lists, Trouble raced around the living room and ran through the pet carrier. She was relaxed and happy; a good sign that she was ready to travel across the country.

The house was a mess. There were piles of stuff everywhere and I could barely walk across the bedroom floor. Although it looked disorganized, I was following my established method of travel preparation. Next to each pile was a plastic bin with a label. Everything would be packed into a bin and organized in the back of the car for easy access during travel. On the floor, Professor had a diagram of the back of the car with the dimensions to make sure all of our stuff would fit in the space.

I got the idea for the bins and labels during one trip to Yellowstone. I was getting something out of our car in the parking lot at the Lake Yellowstone Hotel. A woman opened the hatch of the SUV parked next to us. I couldn't help but notice that the back of the car was full of bins, neatly packed and clearly labeled. She methodically selected a bin, opened it and took out what she needed – no sorting through luggage or taking everything out of the car to find one item.

"Wow, that's impressive!" I exclaimed. I usually keep to myself, but I like to be very organized and am always looking for new ideas.

"It's the only way I can keep track of things," she replied while carefully replacing the lid on the open bin.

I never got the woman's name, but I thank her every time I manage to get our travel supplies neatly organized into bins in the back of the car. Keeping everything organized also saves time and money. When we stop at a rest stop and need a treat or kitty litter, I know where to find it. We don't waste time rifling through all of the stuff in our car or money by having to pay the high prices of the nearest retailer.

At the supermarket, I bought every can of Trouble's favorite food. Looking at the empty shelf, I felt guilty about the next cat owner who would come along looking for this food and find an empty space. Then I thought about how Trouble enjoys eating and how she purrs contentedly when she is devouring her favorite food after traveling in the car. I doublechecked the shelf to make sure I had every can.

"Do you have a lot of cats?" the cashier asked politely, as he scanned 24 cans of cat food.

"No, but my cat really loves this food," I replied, watching the screen as it totaled the cost of the expensive cat food. It was worth the money to keep Trouble satisfied and healthy.

The cashier nodded his head kindly while looking at me like I was a crazy cat lady with hordes of cats.

The day before we left Jacksonville, I woke up with a jolt, lists of things to do running through my mind. I always feel anxious – worried that we will forget something. I have heard stories about people who forgot to turn their refrigerator water dispenser off, flooding the kitchen, or left the stove on, starting a fire. I mull over every item on my lists.

Professor was going back and forth between the bedroom and the car, carrying my neatly-labeled bins. I heard him cursing under his breath.

"What's the matter, Dear?" I asked, anticipating his reply.

"You always pack too much!" he grimaced while staggering under the weight of the bin holding all of the cat food.

"Will everything fit in the car?" I continued, trusting his mathematical abilities and experience. This is our routine; I pack a lot of stuff and he tries to figure out how to squeeze it all in the car. The pet carrier takes up the entire back seat so this reduces the space for our luggage and bins.

"It will fit, but I have to move things around. You will have to put your stuff at your feet. The cat's travel bag will be behind your seat." Professor kept talking as he deftly maneuvered the bin out the door into the garage. I was not listening – too busy thinking about the tasks on my list. I trusted him to engineer the packing so that everything fit in the car and I felt better knowing that we were well-prepared for the trip.

As I reviewed my lists, Trouble curled up in a patch of sunshine next to my feet. She seemed relaxed, but I knew she sensed my anxiety. Once we start packing the car, she knows we are getting ready to leave. Sometimes she shows her displeasure by pooping in different places. Yesterday she pooped next to Professor's chair at the dining room table. I didn't tell him; he gets upset when she goes on the carpet. A pet cleaning product quickly removed the evidence of the accident.

Trouble wandered out onto the sun porch and sat on her favorite chair, watching the birds in the backyard. After years of building gardens, planting trees and maintaining several bird feeders, we have families of cardinals, blue jays, several species of woodpeckers, nuthatches, pine warblers, creepers, chickadees and hawks. A family of Red-Shouldered Hawks have a nest nearby and are responsible for the limited number of squirrels and snakes in our yard.

One of my favorite birds is the Pileated Woodpecker. An endangered species, this bird is a rare sight. The extensive development in Florida has resulted in a loss of the Pileated Woodpecker's habitat. With the current pace of development in our area, I am concerned about this bird's future and feel privileged when the Pileated Woodpecker visits our yard. This large bird, nearly the size of a crow, with a bright red crown, black and white stripes and a large pointed bill, is an impressive sight. This magnificent bird likes to search for bugs in a dead pine tree behind our house. I heard the sounds of his powerful bill tearing large pieces of bark off the tree and then drilling holes in the tree trunk looking for bugs.

Trouble also enjoys watching the birds. Her hunting instincts kick in and she crouches low, watching every movement of the birds going in and out of the feeders. Occasionally, a bird will hop into the bright red ceramic bird bath perched on the edge of the stone wall near the sun porch. This time it was the female cardinal, splashing water, enjoying the feel of clean fresh water on her feathers. Trouble crept slowly up to the screen, stalking the bird. The birds knew that she could not reach them from behind the screen, so they ignored her.

As I watched, Professor took the bird feeders down. Summer thunderstorms in Florida can be severe with winds over 50 miles per hour, so it's best to leave the feeders on the ground. I saw the cardinal family and the blue jay family looking for seed. I felt guilty, but it was summer and they have plenty of choices for food in the forest behind our home.

The next day, it was time to leave. We began our trip early on a Saturday morning to avoid traffic in Jacksonville. We walked through the house, checklists in hand, to make sure everything was put away, turned off and ready for the house sitter. I was feeling stressed; overwhelmed by the thoughts of driving across the country with the cat and leaving our house for three months.

Trouble was also anxious, sensing that she would be leaving soon. She sat under the coffee table in the family room close to the wall, hoping that I could not see her and she could follow her daily routine of playing in the sunroom and sleeping on the couch.

Professor and I crossed off the last item on the check list. I picked up Trouble and put her in the pet carrier. My right hand was on her chest and I felt her heart beating a bit faster than usual, but it was not pounding like when we go to the vet. This was a good sign; she was not feeling too stressed.

We put the pet carrier in the car and worked on making the cat comfortable. I put a clean litter box at one end of the pet carrier, surrounded by puppy pee pads to catch any accidents. I pulled the clean bed sheet over the cat, reminding her to "Settle down." She crawled under the sheet and pulled it around her, disappearing from my sight. I looked at the lump in the sheet and heard Trouble purring; she was ready to leave.

Professor and I got settled in the front seats. As Professor backed the car out of the driveway, a million things popped into my head and I peppered Professor with questions: "Did you turn the stove off?"; "Did you lock the door?"; "Did you email the house sitter?" Professor patiently answered each one of my questions. He's used to dealing with my anxiety.

As we drove across Jacksonville, heading north, I took a deep breath, trying to stop thinking in lists, and checking around the car to make sure everyone was okay. Trouble was yowling, so I turned around and looked inside the carrier. She pushed her face against the mesh. I rubbed her face and she calmed down...for a minute. Then she started yowling again. This was normal; it usually takes her about 15 to 30 minutes to settle down.

I looked at Professor, wiggling around in the driver's seat. He has an infuriating habit of moving around while he gets comfortable – adjusting his clothes, cleaning his glasses, rubbing his eyes. The car weaves back and forth in the highway lane during these antics. Thirty years of pleas to "Watch the road – you're weaving all over the place!" have had no effect. So now I remain quiet while holding onto the door handle and hoping he finishes soon.

Professor settled down in his seat and I breathed a sigh of relief. "Are you comfortable now?" I asked, tersely.

"Yes, I'm very comfortable and so excited to be driving to Montana. I can't wait to get to my favorite hiking trails!"

"Good," I said, looking at the itinerary. I appreciated his energy and enthusiasm, but all I could think about was the long drive across the country.

We sat quietly, listening to the classic rock music that Professor organized for the trip, and watching the traffic. Jacksonville is a very busy city now, unlike the small, quiet city that we moved to 20 years ago.

When we saw the "Thank you for visiting Florida" sign just before crossing the state line into Georgia, I exhaled fully and started to relax. Our journey was officially under way.

Our destination on the first day was North Carolina. We drove through Georgia, stopping to eat lunch and check on Trouble. We followed our established method for cleaning the cat box; a process developed after making mistakes on our first trip and learning from our cat. I cleaned the box, gave Trouble a treat and got back in the car. We were back on the highway with a quiet, content cat within a short time.

When the car crossed the border into South Carolina, I checked the traffic report.

"There's a big accident on I-95 about 20 minutes from our current location," I said, looking at the traffic report on my smart phone. Professor decided to take a detour on a local highway to avoid the accident.

As we drove through the back roads and small towns of South Carolina, I felt like we were going back in time. Many of the homes, both large and small, were reminiscent of the South before the Civil War. Much of it was ramshackle; a testimony to the modern migration of the population to cities.

In one town, we drove by a cotton field. White balls of cotton were strewn across the field, alongside the road and on the railroad tracks running right through the field. I was instantly transported back to a time when cotton was a major industry in the American South. It felt surreal, like being on the set of a movie.

Professor was scowling, pondering something – probably history.

"What are you thinking about?" I asked, expecting a history lecture to follow.

"I was just thinking about my family trips back and forth from Philadelphia, Pennsylvania to Greenville, South Carolina when I was a kid. My family heritage is deeply rooted in the South. During our long car rides to South Carolina, my mother would frequently talk about our family roots and history. As a kid, I didn't listen to her stories. I regret that now since my mother is elderly and suffering from dementia. She doesn't remember the stories."

Professor put the car on cruise control and sat back in his seat before continuing with his story.

"From what I remember, one side of my family tree originates before the United States even existed. My ancestor Abraham was born in 1655. He left Europe because of religious persecution and emigrated to the Virginia Colony. Then generations of his family spread into North Carolina and South Carolina. My ancestor Reuben was wounded at the Battle of Yorktown during the Revolutionary War. Many of my ancestors were lost during the Civil War fighting on both sides – for the Union and the Confederacy."

"That explains why you are always so patriotic. It's in your blood," I said. Professor's pride in being an American is evident in his passion for history.

Professor took a deep breath. "I am proud of my heritage, but some of it is not talked about in our family. It reflects the history of the country – the good parts and the bad parts. Our family tree includes African-American slaves, Native Americans and also slave owners. Some of my ancestors were involved with the relocation of the Cherokee and Creek Indians from their lands in the East to Oklahoma over the infamous Trail of Tears."

"Wow! That's a complicated history."

Professor nodded. After 30 years together, we share each other's thoughts. We rode together in silence, pondering the history of the American South and how it continues to pervade our society today.

Professor drove the car back to the main highway and we headed toward North Carolina. Soon we would arrive at the hotel and begin our step-by-step process for getting the cat secured and settled in a hotel room.

10 BEWARE OF CAT

After driving for six hours, we arrived in Charlotte, North Carolina. Professor pulled the car up to the front entrance of the hotel and jumped out, running inside to get us checked in. As part of the check-in process, he agreed to pay a pet fee of 125 dollars. This is an outrageous amount considering that the "pet rooms" are often in poor condition and not very clean. Many hotels are trying to make extra money from people traveling with their pets.

Trouble sensed the change in activity and climbed out from under the sheet in the corner of her carrier. She pressed her nose against the mesh of the pet carrier, looking at me curiously, wondering what was happening. "We're almost there, sweet kitty," I said, scratching her head through the mesh. She responded with a low grunt. Every time the car stops, Trouble hopes that it's time for her to get out of the carrier.

I was also weary of sitting in the car and it was only the first day of our 10-day trip. I am tall so sitting in the car for many hours causes cramps in my legs and stiffness in my lower back. My neck was stiff from napping in the car so I guessed that the cat also gets stiff and sore from being cooped up in the car.

Professor returned with our hotel room key and we followed our routine for getting the cat settled into a hotel room. The cat is our first priority; everything else comes second. Professor held the pet carrier as I carried the cat's travel bag and litter box. We squeezed into the elevator, leaving little room for other people. As the elevator started moving, Trouble started howling – a distressing sound that makes me feel guilty for taking the cat away from the familiar comforts in our Florida home. Trouble doesn't like elevators.

"It's okay, Trouble; we're almost there," Professor said, reassuringly. The other people in the elevator stared at the pet carrier, visibly upset at the loud cat sounds.

"Our cat doesn't like elevators," Professor explained. They nodded politely but were probably wondering about the crazy people traveling with their noisy cat.

Once we were safely in the hotel room, Professor opened the pet carrier and Trouble jumped out. She raced around the room, inspecting every corner and sniffing loudly to take in all of the new smells. I quickly unpacked Trouble's food and bowl, knowing that she was very hungry. She only eats a small amount of food in the morning, preparing to ride in the car. I believe that during our first trip she probably felt a little nauseous. She adjusted quickly, learning to eat a small meal in the morning and a larger meal in the evening. I placed her bowl of food on the floor and she started gobbling up the food.

"Not too fast, Trouble," I reminded her while stroking her to help her relax. She has a tendency to eat too fast and then her stomach gets upset. I believe this comes from having been a stray cat who never knew where her next meal was coming from.

As I guarded the cat, Professor opened the hotel room door and returned to the car to unpack our luggage and cat supplies. I rummaged around in the cat's bag and found the sign for the hotel room door. "Beware of Cat! Do not open the door," the sign says in bold red letters. The message is repeated in Spanish, with a warning about "el gato." I taped the sign securely to the front of the hotel room door and also hung the "Do Not Disturb" sign from the door knob. The "Beware of Cat" sign is supposed to keep hotel employees from entering the room. Apparently, some people think it's funny since our sign has been stolen from the door on several occasions.

Once our overnight essentials are unpacked, we spend most of our time in the hotel room playing with the cat while relaxing from a long day of driving. In the morning, we leave the room to go to breakfast and restock our supplies at the local supermarket. Leaving the cat alone in the hotel room fills me with extreme uneasiness the entire time we are away from the room.

I have a recurring nightmare. In the nightmare, Trouble is locked securely in the room, with the "Do Not Disturb" sign on the doorknob and the "Beware of Cat" sign on the door. The hotel housekeeper ignores the signs and opens the door. Trouble always runs to the door to greet us, so she is sitting right next to the door. When the door opens, she is scared by the housekeeper's vacuum (Trouble hates vacuum cleaners) and dashes out the door. In the dream, Professor and I step off the elevator into the hallway to see a frantic scene. The cat is running down the hallway, chased by a small boy and the housekeeper. Professor and I join the chase, but Trouble is faster. We can't catch her. I wake up with a jolt, slowly realizing that it's just a nightmare. However, this dream reminds me to be extra careful when we stay in a hotel.

We have never had a problem and our cat has always been safe in hotel rooms, but we take every precaution. I heard a knock on the door. "Is that you, Dear?" I asked, looking out the peephole. Professor was standing close to the door, so all I could see was his red shirt.

"Yes, open the door!" He was tired and cranky from the long day of travel and his patience was at the lowest point of the day.

I locked the cat in the bathroom to keep her safe and opened the door for Professor who wheeled in a luggage cart piled high with our supplies. I worked on unpacking the food and basic necessities while Professor stretched out on the couch and read the paper. He insisted on doing most of the driving so he was exhausted.

Trouble slept during the long car ride so she was full of energy. She ran around the room, jumping on the furniture and inspecting all of the window sills. She climbed around the kitchen – on top of the refrigerator and across the top of the cabinets. Next, she investigated things at the ground level. She went under the bed skirt, behind the curtains, behind the couch and under the television. She was looking for a place to hide in the morning when we started packing the car. Thankfully, this hotel has wood panels around the base of the bed so that Trouble cannot get under or behind the bed.

In the past, we made the mistake of staying in a hotel room with beds whose frames did not block the space underneath the bed. We went down to breakfast in the morning, leaving the cat snoozing on top of the bed and returned from breakfast to find her hiding under the bed. At each hotel, Trouble quickly learned our routine and then developed a strategy to avoid getting back into the pet carrier. We were always trying to stay one step ahead of her, but she outsmarted us.

After dinner, we relaxed in front of the television. I usually read books, but my brain was tired after a long day of travel and so I stared at the home improvement show that Professor and I like to watch. Trouble ate her evening snack and was full of energy. She raced around the hotel room, playing hide and seek; a game we play at home. She hides and jumps out at me as I walk by, pretending I don't know where she is.

I looked up from my book and saw Trouble batting a red rubber ball across the floor. I started laughing and Professor joined me; the cat looked like a kitten playing with the ball. I was glad that she was relaxed and getting some exercise. Suddenly, I realized that we do not own a red rubber ball.

"Where did she find that red ball?" I demanded, jumping up from the couch.

Professor didn't respond because the next minute I was yelling, "Trouble, drop it!" The cat looked at me with a piece of chocolate cookie in her mouth. I yelled again, feeling guilty for scaring her but wanting to make sure she didn't eat the cookie which would make her sick. I grabbed the cookie as she dropped it and ran out of the kitchen. I knelt down on the hard floor and looked under the refrigerator to see if there were more cookies.

"Yuck! It's filthy! The floor underneath the refrigerator is covered with bits of food and trash. No wonder Trouble keeps finding food," I continued, angrily. "We pay pet fees so that the room is very clean. Instead, the trash is being swept under the furniture."

After this incident, Professor and I adopted the term "hotel treasure" to refer to all of the things that Trouble finds under the furniture and appliances in hotel rooms. She learned to look for food under the refrigerator so I had to block access to it in every hotel room. She learned that there is stuff behind the bed and under the couch. I force myself to look in these spaces, never knowing what I will find. I found all kinds of things including a baby's pacifier and a condom.

It makes me angry that we pay extra money to stay in these rooms at international hotel brands and they are often disgusting. One time we were given a room with worn-out furniture and appliances that didn't work right. This was in a hotel that was otherwise very nice. Clearly many of the hotels do not maintain the pet rooms to the same standards as the rest of the hotel, while charging extra fees for the pets.

After one disappointing hotel stay, I sent an email to the hotel's general manager. I received a very professional reply including a promise of improvement on our next stay. We stayed at the hotel on our next trip and were given a room that was even worse than our original room. After that, we didn't complain for fear of retaliation.

Trouble is a fastidious cat. She uses her litter box consistently and I clean up any stray litter and throw out the box before we leave. Anyone entering the room would not be able to tell that a cat had stayed there.

"This makes me crazy," I fumed. "We paid a 125-dollar pet fee and the room is not clean!"

"What can we do? We have to stay in a pet room. We don't have a lot of choices for hotels that take pets on this trip." Professor was right, but it didn't make me feel any better.

"I know, but it still makes me mad." I paced up and down the living room, feeling frustrated.

The next morning, we woke up early so that Trouble could have her breakfast and relax before traveling. We got on the road early, while the weather was clear and the traffic was light. We were heading to Mom and Dad's house in Ohio for a couple of days of rest and family visits.

11 THE LITTER BOX ROUTINE

Our second day of traveling followed a familiar pattern. Professor drove the car through the mountains of North Carolina, enjoying the scenery. I tried to read a book while worrying about every detail of the trip. Trouble was snoring underneath the sheet in her carrier with a subtle, nasal sound.

Professor sniffed loudly, "Do you smell something?"

"No, I don't smell anything."

Professor sniffed again. "I think the cat used the litter box."

A few minutes later, we heard Trouble scratching her claws in the litter box. The strong smell of cat poop pervaded the air inside the car.

"Wow – that stinks!" I said, quickly opening the window to let fresh air in to clear out the smell.

Professor was speaking, but I couldn't hear what he was saying. Trouble was howling loudly and persistently; she wanted her box cleaned immediately.

"We need to find a place to pull over so we can clean the cat's box," I shouted to Professor who was already turning the car toward the next exit.

Trouble is a finicky cat. She is fastidious and won't go near the box if it's dirty or smells. Finding a reliable method to manage the litter box in the car took considerable time and patience. We learned to interpret all of her various sounds – howls, yowls, grunts and meows along with her behavior.

After trial and error, we realized that she preferred having the litter box in one end of the carrier. Trouble mastered the art of using her box while the car was moving. When the box was dirty, she would yowl until it was clean.

As Professor pulled the car into a parking space at the rest stop, the cat howled even louder to get our full attention. Professor and I jumped out of the car, happy to breathe fresh air and to give our ears a break from the noise. We opened the rear passenger doors with Professor on the driver's side and me on the passenger side. We followed our established Litter Box Routine to avoid making mistakes and to keep the cat relaxed.

The Litter Box Routine looks like this:

- Professor opens the zipper on his side of the pet carrier and hooks a leash on to the cat's collar. She's skittish; a loud motorcycle or truck could easily scare her. The leash prevents her from jumping out of the pet carrier and the car.

- He lifts up the piece of cardboard lying in the middle of the carrier, blocking the cat's path to my side of the carrier.

- Once the cat is secure, I open the opposite end of the pet carrier to access the litter box. I have organized the litter box with layers of puppy pee pads and cat litter. I quickly lift the top pad, bringing the soiled litter with it and leaving the next layer of clean litter. Trouble will continue to yowl if the box is the slightest bit dirty.

The Litter Box Routine only takes a few minutes. Professor pets Trouble and talks to her while I clean the box.

"Okay, I'm done," I said, after zipping up my side of the pet carrier.

"You're all done?" Professor responded, making sure my end of the pet carrier was closed before he took the leash off the cat.

"Yes, I'm finished," I repeated, wiping my hands with an antibacterial cleaner. I heard Trouble purring loudly, content now that her box was clean and she knew her good behavior would be rewarded.

"Here's a treat, Trouble," Professor said. I heard the crunching sound of the cat chewing on the treat. She was still purring and would settle down for a nap once we got back on the highway.

We developed the Litter Box Routine after making many mistakes.

One time, I opened the car door and Trouble almost jumped out of the car. She had pulled at the mesh on the end of the carrier and opened the zipper. I reacted quickly, catching her by the collar with one hand while pulling the zipper up with the other hand. Only after I pushed the cat back into the pet carrier and secured the zipper did I think about what might have happened.

"The cat almost got out!" I yelled to Professor, who was standing on the other side of the car. I was hysterical thinking about what might have happened if she had escaped from the car into the busy parking lot. She would have been scared from all of the noise. When Trouble is scared, she runs and hides. She would have run straight for the patch of woods next to the parking lot and we would never have been able to catch her.

During our first trip to Bozeman, we tried to get her to use the litter box on a schedule. Each morning, we went to breakfast at the hotel hoping she would use the litter box in the room before we got in the car. Instead, she hid under the bed or behind the curtains. We returned to the hotel room to find an anxious cat who refused to use her box.

On that first trip, we only put the litter box in the pet carrier when we stopped at a rest stop. We figured the cat would use it in privacy while we stood outside the car stretching. Instead, Trouble would yowl and claw the sides of the pet carrier, thinking it was time for her to get out of the car.

We kept trying to find ways to get the cat to use her box while we were on the road. We were determined to find a solution to the litter box usage dilemma. We had only been successful in getting Trouble to use her box in the hotel when we arrived in the afternoon. I would place it in a quiet corner where she would use it immediately, clearly showing us that she'd been waiting a while to do her business. We realized that we had more work to do in finding the ideal solution.

We had faced this issue once before. When Trouble first became a house cat, she did not always use her litter box, preferring the fuzzy carpet. After trying different types of boxes, litter and pheromones which were supposed to relax the cat, we took her to the veterinarian.

I sat in the exam room while the veterinarian put x-rays on the viewing screen and explained the cat's anatomy. I tried to focus on the biology lesson, but I was too anxious. In a short time, Trouble had rooted herself deeply within my heart and I wanted nothing more than this adorable, sweet kitty to live a long, healthy life. It was incredibly difficult to listen to the doctor review all of the things that might be wrong with my new buddy. My anxiety rose with each uncomfortable possibility.

"Trouble has a high percentage of struvite crystals in her urine," the veterinarian explained while looking at the manila folder in her hands, unaware that I was not paying attention.

"Struvites?" I repeated, realizing that I had missed the biology lesson.

"Yes," the veterinarian replied and then continued with her explanation of struvites, making them sound like an alien that had invaded my cat's digestive system. "She may also have a urinary tract infection. I'll prescribe an antibiotic." The struvites and infection appeared to be the cause of Trouble's box-avoiding behavior.

When Trouble did not use the litter box regularly during our first trip, I wondered if the struvites were the source of the problem. "I'm worried that Trouble is avoiding the litter box because she has an infection," I said as we left our hotel room one morning.

Professor, as usual, was not worried. "We will keep trying until we find something that works."

"I'm out of ideas," I replied sharply, tired from traveling and wishing we were already in Bozeman so the cat and I could relax into our summer schedule.

"Maybe she would be happier in the fresh air," he said, thoughtfully. I nodded, allowing Professor to be creative and generate new ideas.

During that trip, we were driving through rural Missouri, surrounded by farmland and few rest stops. I saw a sign for an exit that said "Crane's

Museum and Shops/Marlene's Restaurant."

"Pull off here," I said, pointing to the exit.

Professor pulled the car into the parking lot for Crane's Museum and Shops/Marlene's Restaurant. The parking lot was full of dusty pickup trucks and our SUV was the only one like it in the parking lot. As we sat in the car deciding what to do, several men came out of the restaurant. They were wearing plaid shirts, dusty jeans, suspenders and stained John Deere caps.

I grew up in dairy farm country in Upstate New York so this scene looked familiar. "I guess the farmers are having a late breakfast," I said. "I'm sure they're wondering what city-slickers like us are doing here."

Professor nodded, smiling at my attempt at a joke. He grew up in suburban Philadelphia so he was not used to seeing groups of farmers and he wasn't sure what to expect from this restaurant.

We decided to leave the cat in the car with the windows open to let in the spring breeze. The place was very quiet and we hoped Trouble would relax and use the litter box which we had just placed in the carrier.

Professor and I went inside Marlene's Restaurant and were overwhelmed by the smells of pastries and coffee. We relaxed at a table while the friendly waitress poured our coffee and served fresh baked goods. I kept having flashbacks to being in my grandmother's house – feeling the warmth of a well-loved place with the scent of fresh baked pie, coffee and a hint of the musty smell of antiques.

We were reluctant to leave the warm atmosphere in Marlene's Restaurant, but we needed to check on our cat and get back on the road. Trouble was sitting peacefully on one side of the pet carrier, smelling the fresh air, filled with the scent of clover and freshly plowed dirt, but she had not used the box.

Professor suggested that we put the pet carrier in the park next to the restaurant. It seemed crazy, but we were desperate to find a way to get the cat to use her litter box. Professor lifted the pet carrier out of the car and put it down in the grass nearby. He held on to Trouble while I put the litter box in the other end of the pet carrier. We stood next to the pet carrier not speaking, just looking at each other with raised eyebrows and hopeful expressions.

The cat walked over to the box, sniffed the litter and put one paw in to test it. I looked up and saw a group of farmers standing nearby, chatting and occasionally glancing our way. There was no doubt that they were wondering what we were doing, standing and staring at a large black tunnel lying in the grass in the park.

"What do you think those farmers are saying?" I asked Professor.

His parents grew up on farms in South Carolina. Speaking with a Southern accent which sounded like his father's accent, Professor said, "Homer, looks like a couple of crazy city-slickers. Whaddaya think they've got in that black tube thingy on the grass?"

He continued in a slightly different voice, "Haven't the faintest idea, Jeb, but sure sounds like they've got some critter in there kicking up a ruckus."

Professor's attempt at humor struck just the right chord to ease the tension. I started laughing at his silly impersonations. Having grown up in a small town with lots of dairy farmers, I could imagine how crazy we looked from their point of view.

As my laughter persisted, Professor started laughing, too: a contagious chuckle that he inherited from his father. Sensing our mood shift, Trouble joined the fun by purring loudly. I looked down at her; she was standing with her nose pressed to the mesh fabric of the carrier, sniffing and following the movements of a butterfly fluttering over a nearby flower. She had not used her litter box and seemed to have no intention of doing so.

Even though I was still worried about the cat not using her box, I simply could not stop laughing. Professor now looked at me with a concerned expression. He figured I was starting to lose my grip on my sanity from the long days of travel and fussing over the cat. Hysteria took over as all I could think about was how ridiculous we must have looked to those farmers. It's not every day that they get to see city-folk standing in the middle of a field staring down at a pet carrier anxiously waiting for a cat to use her litter box. I'm sure we were quite a spectacle.

Professor and I were now doubled over in hysterical laughter, unable to control ourselves as we thought about the whole situation. I caught sight of one of the farmers perplexedly shaking his head as he climbed back into his truck. I hoped we had provided some entertainment on an otherwise quiet morning.

Trouble never used her litter box while we were on the road that day. She waited until we arrived at the hotel that afternoon. This trend continued during our first trip to Montana. As a result, we ended up in dire circumstances. We misunderstood what Trouble was trying to communicate; what she wanted was the litter box to be placed in the carrier where it was convenient.

I sighed as I finished my mental review of that stressful time with Trouble. We had come a long way since that first trip.

12 COAL MINER'S GREAT-GRANDDAUGHTER

We continued our current trip, driving toward Mom and Dad's house in Ohio. As we drove through the mountains of Virginia, I stared out the window, watching the scenery change. I noticed the change in light as we drove near the Blue Ridge Mountains in Virginia; the mountains appeared to be a dusky shade of blue.

We crossed the state line into West Virginia and the scenery changed again. West Virginia has the Allegheny and Blue Ridge Mountain ranges. The car shifted right and left as we wound through the mountains. West Virginia has beautiful views but also has many peaks that look more like the mesas that we see out west – flat on top. The tops of the mountains are bare. On a windy day, clouds of dust blow across the mountains, obscuring the view. The barren mountaintops appear sad and lonely – no trees, flowers, animals or other critters.

The flat-topped mountains are remnants of mountaintop removal coal mining. As much as I despair at seeing the tops of mountains blown away and left to erode further in the elements, I am reminded that coal mining played an important role in my family's history. During the early 1900's, coal mining sustained my ancestors and was ultimately responsible for my great-grandfather's death.

We stopped at a gas station to see to our cat's needs. Trouble licked my hand after she ate her treat and then buried under her sheet. She was a model traveler so far. Professor pulled the car back on to the highway and we passed a billboard advertising the coal industry.

"I've been in a coal mine," I said loudly, talking over the classic rock music that was blaring from the car stereo.

"When was that?" Professor turned down the volume on the stereo.

"I visited Wales when I was in college and we went on a tour of a coal mine. I remember crawling on my hands and knees through a narrow tunnel.

I was wearing a helmet with a light, but it was so dark that I could barely see the person in front of me. I kept scraping my helmet on the low ceiling."

"I'm guessing that you didn't like crawling through a coal mine." Professor knows I get claustrophobic in elevators and can't sleep without at least one light on in the bedroom.

"I felt very claustrophobic, especially when they insisted that we turn off the lights. The total darkness was scary; I couldn't see my hand in front of my face. It made me think about my great-grandfather, working in coal mines his whole life."

"Your great-grandfather was a coal miner? I didn't know that. So that means Grandma grew up in a coal mining town and you are a coal miner's great-granddaughter."

I paused for a moment, thinking about Professor's words. "Yes, that's right; although I don't usually think of myself in that way. Coal mining is part of my ancestry; the dust is mixed into my DNA."

"Since we are driving through coal mining country, and have plenty of time to talk, you should tell me all about it." Professor put the car on cruise-control and leaned back in his seat.

I started talking, thinking about my grandmother and losing myself in the story as the car sped through the mountains of West Virginia. Grandma was a special person. Recently, Mom gave me a photo of Grandma holding me when I was six months old. I was smiling and looking up at Grandma with my bright blue eyes. Even when I was a baby, Grandma was one of my favorite people.

Grandma always found joy in the simple things; a big hug was enough to make her smile and laugh. On her 75th birthday, we surprised her with a family party. Her expression of love and delight was captured in the photo that Professor took when we all yelled, "Surprise!" as Grandma walked into the house.

Grandma liked to spread her loving kindness to everyone she met. Even when a car mechanic took advantage of her, charging too much money for basic car repairs, she spoke kindly about him. "He was a nice young man," she said while smiling.

I wished I had taken more time to listen to Grandma's stories about growing up in a coal mining town in the early 1900's. When I was a kid, it just seemed to be part of the conversation. Now I have to rely on what I can remember from Grandma's stories and my own research. Grandma shared some of her memories with me and gave me letters which she had written to her mother after she left home to get married at age 17.

Grandma was born and raised in Dante, a coal mining town in Southwest Virginia in the Appalachian Mountains. Her father, my great-grandfather, worked in the coal mines until he died from "black lung" disease; a disease suffered by miners after years of working in the coal mines. Black lung occurs when the coal dust builds up in the lungs, slowly killing the lung tissue, until the person suffocates, causing a slow, painful death.

In the early 20th century, Dante was a "company town." This meant that the main reason for the town was to support the miners and their families. Most men worked in the mines and the community revolved around mining. The coal mining company owned most of the businesses and buildings, including the homes where the miners lived. Churches, schools and libraries were built to encourage healthy communities and productive workers. Many workers were paid with company "script" – a credit which could only be spent at the Company Store. The Company Store was often the only store in town, carrying the household necessities for the miners and their families. The prices were high since there was no competition. A mine employee could not leave his job without paying off his credit from the Company Store.

Large families were common. Choices were limited since contraceptives were generally unavailable or illegal and a topic that was not discussed in public. Grandma said her "Daddy was a sexy man." Her father apparently had energy left over after working long hours in the coal mine. Her mother gave birth to 14 children and Grandma was the oldest living child. Her older sister died of pneumonia as a toddler. "She went out in the snow in her bare feet and then got sick," Grandma told me. When I looked at the history of that time, this was during the 1918 Flu Pandemic when an estimated 50 million people died.

Coal miners' families often lived below the poverty line. For a poor family, raising 13 children would have put tremendous strain on the family's budget. Women had gardens, did mending for other families, and found all kinds of ways to stretch the family's income. Children often worked in the mines. Child labor was not regulated until the Fair Labor Standards Act was passed in 1938. A 10-year-old boy could go into narrow mine passages too small for adult men. The boy's wages would help ease the family's financial strain.

Family life was difficult. In the early 20th century, before labor laws limited what a company could require of its workers, men often worked 12-hour shifts, 6 days a week. Women did not usually work outside the home. Taking care of the house, the garden, cooking for the family and caring for the kids was a full-time job. Most houses did not have indoor plumbing. The bathroom was in the outhouse which may have had several seats to accommodate two or three people at one time.

In the stories from those people who grew up in Dante in the early 20th century, people said that they realize now that they were poor, but at the time they did not feel poor. That was just the way things were. Similarly, Grandma rarely complained about having very little, except for having to spend hours "picking stones out of the dried beans." She talked about the time there was a "big snake in the outhouse" and she had to get her brother to kill it. She told me how she "ruined a favorite yellow dress" when no one bothered to tell her about puberty and the facts of life.

Grandma never complained about going hungry or not having enough possessions or new clothes. Even though she was financially poor for most of her life and had few personal possessions by today's standards, she was always satisfied with what she had.

For women, running a household was labor intensive including washing laundry by hand, and cooking over an open fire or old wood stove. Cleaning was heavy labor; the only modern convenience being a broom. Clothes were often handmade and then handed down from older siblings because new clothes were too expensive. Young Grandma was taught to be an excellent seamstress and she continued making clothes for herself and family until late in life. She even made Mom's wedding gown.

Children were expected to help around the house starting at an early age – carrying water, pulling weeds in the garden, chopping wood, hunting for small game. Water for cooking, drinking and washing was hauled from a local stream. There were no environmental regulations at that time, so no one worried about the streams having contamination from the mines. They were content to have a source of water.

Grandma always referred to the refrigerator as the "icebox." I realize now that her childhood home would have had an actual icebox. A predecessor to the refrigerator, the icebox kept food cold without electricity by using real ice which was delivered to households in big blocks.

In a company town, families often struggled to survive. As the oldest of 13 children, crammed into a house that would be lived in by a family of four in the 21st century, young Grandma was treated as an adult while she was still in grade school. She had tremendous responsibility. While her mother, was busy taking care of the younger children and having more babies, including twin boys, young Grandma looked after her father and the older children.

"My mother was too busy having babies," Grandma told me at one point, a hint of resentment in her voice.

I imagined that young Grandma's day may have looked like this:

4 a.m. - Wake up and stoke the coal furnace and make breakfast. Give her father his lunch pail as he leaves to work a 12-hour shift at the mine.

5 a.m. - Pack lunch pails for school-aged kids. Eat lukewarm grits and a cold biscuit.

7 a.m. - Walk to school with her siblings.

3:30 p.m. - Arrive home from school and do homework. Grandma graduated from high school; an achievement for a girl in the mountains of Virginia in the 1930's. Many girls got married before finishing high school.

5 p.m. - Do chores around the house and help her mother with dinner. Eat dinner in shifts since the table was not big enough for the whole family.

7 p.m. - Clean up dinner and help the younger kids get ready for bed. Fall

exhausted into bed.

Young Grandma adored her father and was happy to make sure his meals were ready and his lunch pail was packed so he didn't go hungry during his long shift at the mine. Working in a coal mine was, and still is, a dangerous job. Injuries and deaths were a constant reality. When a siren went off, everyone in the town knew that there had been an accident. People would drop whatever they were doing and rush out into the street to try to get the news. "What happened? Was anyone hurt? Who is it? Is anyone dead?" Women would pray that their husbands and sons were alive and uninjured.

Grandma felt very close to her father even after she got married and moved to Long Island. When her father died from black lung disease after decades of working in the mines, Grandma knew it immediately. She was in the basement of her home and burst into tears for no apparent reason. "I didn't know until later, but that was the exact time that my father died," she told me, tearfully.

Young Grandma met my grandfather through her cousin when she was finishing high school. She aspired to be a nurse so she could help people, but she did not have money for nursing school. Young Grandma was married at age 17 and moved to Long Island to live with young Grandpa's relatives while he worked as a chef.

Grandma always lived frugally. She always worked, starting with a job as a hairdresser after she was married. "One woman paid me a quarter even though I only charged $0.15," she wrote gleefully in one letter. Later she worked at Woolworth's and then B. Altman & Company. She managed to save an impressive amount of money while raising three boys, supporting Grandpa's spending habits and occasionally splurging on a new dress for church.

Dante had a strong community bound by the common thread of the coal mines. The church was a focal point of activities. Young Grandma was on the list of the members of the "Friendly Society," having worked on quilts to donate to others in need. This pattern continued throughout Grandma's life. She was a caring person, thoughtful of others' needs and generous even when she only had a little to give.

Grandma had a strong faith throughout her life. "I love you and miss you," she would say on the phone and in her weekly letters to me when I was in college. "I wish I lived closer, but I know God is watching over you and keeping you safe from harm."

Sundays were usually reserved for church and family gatherings. Grandma's letter to her mother said that she missed having "the gang" over for dinner. She also listed some foods that she missed – her mother's homemade pickles, corn muffins and sweet potatoes, which were apparently too expensive in New York.

Sitting around the family radio listening to programs provided hours of entertainment before televisions were available. Grandma's letter to her mother asks about a radio program. "What's happening in '*We Live Again*?' I can't get that show up here in New York."

On special occasions, the entire community would get together for some old-fashioned fun. Grandma's father was a square dance caller and he played the harmonica. Square dances allowed members of the opposite sex to interact in public and gave the community an excuse to take time away from work and chores to have a grand time.

I finished talking about my ancestors and sat silently in the car, pondering my family history. Despite the dramatic differences in lifestyle, I have a lot in common with my ancestors. They lived in poverty in a coal mining town and our 21st century middle class lifestyle seems luxurious by comparison. However, many of their values have been passed down through the generations. My strong work ethic has always motivated me to push forward, work harder and try to improve in everything that I do. Even when I was in elementary school, I made money by selling seed packets door-to-door in my neighborhood.

I learned to appreciate the simple things in life. Even though I am writing this book 100 years after Grandma was born and society has changed dramatically in that time, the things that really matter in life have not changed. Grandma always signed her letters with "All my love." That says it all.

"Family history is a good reminder of what's really important," I said, breaking the silence.

"Why do you say that?" Professor asked, as he slowed down to read the road signs.

"I'm just thinking about my family history and Grandma. We can learn a great deal from our ancestors."

As I spoke, we left West Virginia and a "Welcome to Ohio" sign greeted us. The next stop was Mom and Dad's house.

13 MOLLY AND TROUBLE

As we pulled into the driveway of my parents' home in Ohio, I exhaled loudly and forcefully. I was glad to have a break from staying in hotels, but also had misgivings about staying with my parents.

"Why are you sighing like that?" Professor asked, turning the car off.

"Staying with my parents feels stressful sometimes." I was taking deep breaths and moving my head slowly to loosen the kinks that had built up in my neck while riding in the car for two days. "It makes me feel like a teenager again – always being told what to do."

"It will be fine." Professor loves my parents and enjoys staying in their house. He cooks dinner and makes delicious desserts, enjoying the opportunity to please everyone with his culinary creations. "It's far better than staying in a hotel."

"You're right about that. At least we can visit family, eat our own food and sleep in a quiet room. We can relax and get caught up on our sleep." We have stayed in some hotels that were so noisy, we felt like we were sleeping in the middle of a busy freeway. I pushed the negative thoughts aside as I saw my parents coming out of the house to greet us.

Trouble realized the car had stopped and crawled out of her cocoon of sheets. She pressed her face against the black mesh of the pet carrier with a soft "Meow?" This was her way of asking, "Are we there yet?"

"Yes, Trouble, we're at Mom and Dad's house," I said. "You always like staying here." She sniffed loudly as I opened the car door, letting the fresh spring air inside the car. Trouble heard the commotion as Professor got out of the car to hug my parents. The cat started yowling loudly, letting us know that she wanted to be taken out of the car – immediately.

"Hello, Trouble." Dad pushed his face against the pet carrier. Trouble recognized him and ran to greet him, sniffing his face and purring softly. Dad adores cats so he greets Trouble first.

The cat always gets priority, so we unloaded the pet carrier and Trouble. We let her out of the carrier in the master bedroom, where we would sleep for the next few days. It's the only room that's big enough for Professor, me and the cat. I worked on getting the cat settled while Professor unloaded our luggage and supplies. Trouble was very hungry since she had only eaten a small breakfast.

"Okay, my sweet cat," I said, rubbing behind her ears to reassure her. "Food is coming." Trouble kept winding around my legs and licking my ankles. She tries to be cute and adorable to make sure I don't do anything else until I give her some food.

I gave Trouble a bowl of food and water in her favorite blue saucepan. She won't drink water out of anything else. The curious thing is that we originally bought this pot on a camping trip to Yellowstone National Park in Montana long before Trouble joined our family. I stood next to her while she gobbled up her food, thinking about this interesting connection. I placed both the dish and the pot on a paper towel to make sure the carpet stayed clean. I don't like doing this since Trouble will eat any dried bits of food that are on the paper towel, consuming pieces of paper along with the food. However, in my parents' house we must be very tidy. Mom obsesses about cleanliness so we do our best to leave everything as we found it.

As Trouble ate her food, I checked the door to the bedroom to make sure it was closed so Trouble couldn't get out of the bedroom. My parents have a cat, Molly, and I worry that the two cats might start fighting. Trouble always fought with other cats when she was an outdoor cat. Standing near the door, I could hear Professor chatting with my parents in the kitchen. He was cooking dinner and already sounded relaxed. My parents say they love having us visit, especially since we cook three hot meals every day. Their actions say something different; it's obvious that we disturb their routine. After a couple of days, they are both out of sorts.

When we visit, my parents sleep in other rooms – Mom in the guest room and Dad in the spare bedroom in the basement. Dad created his own lair in the basement with his model trains. Dad spends hours working on the trains, building entire communities of miniature buildings, people, bridges and mountains around the tracks.

Trouble finished her food and jumped up onto the bench in front of the window. I stood next to her, petting her head while she stared intently out the window. The window looks out on the backyard which is full of Mom's flowers. Perennials line the fence and all kinds of annuals – petunias, pansies, and impatiens, are grouped in pots on the deck. The birdfeeders captured Trouble's attention; busy with the constant activity from cardinals, blue jays, woodpeckers, starlings, sparrows and chickadees. Later in the evening, an owl serenaded us.

The bench Trouble sat on was previously used with an electric organ.

When I was in elementary school, I took organ lessons from a gray-haired, heavy set lady – Mrs. Gray. She spent her days playing the organ, doing complicated jigsaw puzzles and smoking cigarettes. Mrs. Gray's favorite music was popular tunes from the 1940's and 1950's, so that music was the focus of my lessons. To this day, I know all of the words to many songs from that era including Broadway show tunes. Mrs. Gray could play them expertly on the organ, but I just never had the knack. I played in church one time and I was so nervous I could barely make it through the first stanza of the hymn.

Eventually, the organ was donated to a local church. Mom kept the organ bench because she thought it was "a nice piece of furniture." Now the organ bench functions as a cat perch. Trouble sat comfortably on the blue blanket Mom laid across the wooden bench. Molly usually sits here and Mom says she won't sit there again until the blanket has been washed clean of Trouble's scent. Cats can be very particular.

Molly reminds me of a small lion with long, fuzzy, brown and black fur giving the effect of a fluffy mane around her face. My parents found Molly on a cold, rainy Saturday afternoon as they were leaving a shopping mall. Dad walked over to a dumpster to throw out the wrapper from his sandwich. He heard a soft mewling sound behind the dumpster. Looking behind the dumpster, he found a tiny, wet, bedraggled kitten – so tiny it fit in the palm of Dad's hand.

"Look what I found!" Dad exclaimed, picking up the tiny creature. The kitten immediately snuggled into Dad's warm hand.

"Oh, who would leave a kitten like that! The poor thing!" Mom said, joining Dad to peer down at the shivering kitten.

"We should take this kitten home; otherwise it will die." Dad couldn't bear the thought of returning the tiny cat to its spot by the dumpster.

"We can't have another cat; one is enough." Mom was adamant. They had Smoky, a mature gray, short-haired cat who was a former stray with a number of health issues.

"How can we just leave the kitten here?" Dad replied, getting upset.

"Someone else will take it, I'm sure." Mom won the argument. They got into their car and headed home, the kitten's sad eyes watching their car lights leave the parking lot.

A mile down the road, Mom and Dad were seized with guilt. They turned the car around, picked up the kitten and drove home. My niece named the cat "Molly" after a favorite doll. Molly was a timid, sickly kitten – afraid of everyone and everything. Any unusual sound or a quick movement would send Molly scampering down the stairs to the basement where she would hide in the rafters. Dad had to climb up to get her, cuddling her and reassuring her that it was "okay."

Back then, Molly was very thin and was finicky about food. Mom tried many brands of cat food until she found one that Molly liked. Still, Molly had trouble digesting the food. The vet put Molly on a special diet for several months until she started to gain weight. Once she was healthy, Molly settled into my parents' home very quickly. A playful six-month-old kitten, Molly looked to Smoky, a middle-aged, overweight cat for entertainment. Molly would hide around a corner, stalking the older cat. Smoky would come lumbering around the corner, seemingly unaware that Molly was waiting for her. Molly would spring from her hiding place, jump on top of Smoky and ride on her back like a cowboy on a bronco, until Smoky lost patience and shook the kitten off her back.

I was the first one to meet Smoky while I was visiting Mom and Dad. I opened the front door one morning to let the sun come in and saw a short-haired grey cat sitting on the door mat. She appeared to be healthy, well-groomed and de-clawed. She was very thin and craved food and attention. We gave the cat some food and being a smart cat, she returned the next day, and the next day. We made inquiries around the neighborhood, but no one had information about this cat.

Soon my parents became attached to the cat. Mom said the cat reminded her of a cat that she had as a child – Smoky. After a trip to the vet for a checkup and flea treatment, Smoky became a permanent member of the household.

When Smoky died a few years ago after a serious illness, my parents and Molly mourned her loss. Molly would sit in her favorite hiding place, expecting Smoky to come along any minute. When Smoky didn't appear, Molly would lie down with her head between her paws – for hours.

Now the only cat in the house, Molly is pampered and spoiled. She is still finicky about her food. If she doesn't like what is in the dish, Mom empties it and refills it with a different kind of food. Molly doesn't like drinking water out of a cat bowl, so she has a small fountain that makes pleasant waterfall sounds and keeps the water very fresh.

"Has she been drinking from the fountain?" I asked Mom.

"No, but I'm sure she will," Mom said, defending the high cost of the fountain. I never saw Molly drink out of the fountain. She preferred drinking water from the giant dog bowl that sat near the stairs to the basement.

Molly follows Dad everywhere and they hang out together in the basement. When Dad is in the kitchen, Molly sits on the top step of the stairs to the basement and cries softly and persistently, "meow, meow, meow!" Molly sounds like a newborn kitten in contrast to Trouble's loud ear-splitting yowls.

"I'm not coming down to the basement right now, Molly," Dad says, as if he understands what the cat is saying. "She wants me to come downstairs and play," he explained in response to my raised eyebrows. Molly seemed to understand what Dad said and she scampered down the stairs to the basement to pout, sitting on her favorite perch in the rafters.

Later, I joined Molly in the basement so Dad could show me the newest section of his model railroad. Molly sat in the middle of the train tracks, purring contentedly. We have a photo of Molly that we titled "Catzilla." In the photo, Molly sits next to miniature people who make up the communities scattered around the train tracks. Next to the tiny figures, Molly looks like a giant monster. She seems to be aware of her nickname because she likes to steal things – plastic people, light poles, miniature barns and houses, and hide them. Dad says he has never found her secret hiding spot; somewhere in the house is a pile of things that Molly has stolen from the model railroad.

I looked at Molly and she stared back at me. She seemed to say, "I rule this house; don't mess with me." Molly is the queen of the house and she likes it that way, just like Trouble rules over our home.

Later, Professor and I were in the bedroom getting Trouble settled down and trying to relax; we were all weary from traveling. The door to the bedroom was closed tightly. As I lay on the bed reading my book, I heard a soft "swish, swish, swish" on the door. I looked for Trouble – she was sitting by the bed, looking at the door. I opened the door; there was no one there so I went back to reading my book. A few minutes later, I heard "swish, swish, swish" again. I ran to the door and opened it; no one was there.

"We must have a ghost," I said. Professor nodded, mostly ignoring me while he read his book. Trouble's ears perked up so I knew she heard the noise.

The next time I heard the "swish, swish, swish," Trouble ran to the door and stuck her paws into the space between the bottom of the door and the carpet. I followed her, laid down on the floor and looked under the door where I could see a patch of Molly's fluffy fur. Molly was the ghost.

"That's what Molly does when she wants to come inside the bedroom. She brushes her paws on the door." Mom explained in the morning. "Maybe we should see what happens when we put Molly and Trouble together."

"No!" I yelled, thinking about how Trouble used to get into fights with the neighborhood cats when she was an outdoor cat. "Trouble is very territorial; she hates other cats in her space." I imagined Trouble chasing after Molly, who is very timid and does not have any claws. Even the sound of the doorbell sends Molly running to the basement to hide in the rafters.

Even though Molly misses Smoky, she is not completely alone. She plays with the neighbors' cats and stray cats through the screen on the sun porch. There are a lot of cats in this neighborhood.

Professor and I were able to rest and relax while we stayed at Mom and Dad's house. All too soon, it was time to continue our trip to Bozeman, Montana.

14 SNEAKERS AND MOONSHINE

We prepared to leave Mom and Dad's house with mixed emotions. As Professor strapped Trouble's carrier into the back seat of the car and I hugged Mom and Dad, we talked about the long day of driving ahead of us. We were anxious to get to Montana but still had to drive through a number of states to reach our final destination. Trouble was relaxed and she seemed to understand that it was time to continue on our trip.

I looked out the car window as we drove through Indiana and Illinois, the scenery flashing by at 70 miles per hour. Professor was singing along with his favorite classic rock song on the radio and Trouble was buried under her sheet. I heard the gentle sounds of her snoring, so I knew she was okay.

This was our third day of driving and I was tired of traveling. We were driving through the Midwestern states, surrounded by miles of corn, wheat and soybean fields. In every direction, I saw the same thing – flat farm fields, no hills and few trees. When we stopped at a gas station for a break, we were greeted by an expanse of black pavement – no shade trees. We had to leave the car running with the air conditioning on to keep the cat cool while we took turns going inside to the convenience store.

One of the disadvantages of traveling with the cat is that we are always tied to our car. Stopping at a restaurant for lunch is not an option. We pack our lunch and snacks and eat at a picnic table or in the car. Eating sandwiches and snacks on a long car trip reminds me of family trips that we took when my sisters and I were young.

As Professor pulled the car back onto the highway, he glanced at me, slouched in the front passenger seat. "How are you doing?"

"I hate long car rides," I said, shifting in my seat and stretching my shoulders. My back and shoulders were already feeling stiff after sitting for two hours in the car.

"I know driving through farm fields is not exciting, but think about how important this corn, wheat and soy is to our country." Professor is always very sage, taking an expansive view of an uncomfortable situation. "These farmers and their fields provide food for millions of people and animals around the world."

I nodded my head, fully appreciating the importance of corn, wheat and soybeans. History offers a perspective on what would happen if we did not have these farms. I recently read John Steinbeck's book, *The Grapes of Wrath* for a second time. The award-winning book provides insight into what could happen if we did not have all of these prosperous farms.

"Let me tell you why I loathe long car rides." I shifted in my seat once again before beginning my story.

Professor nodded his head, leaned back in his seat, put the car on cruise control and waited patiently for me to begin my story. I thought about my experiences for a bit before beginning the tale.

My family, including Mom, Dad and my sisters, took many trips when I was young. These trips involved spending long hours cramped in the back seat of a car with my two sisters. One car, a red Dodge Omni, was a compact hatchback designed to be fuel-efficient during a time when gas prices were very high. However, the car was not designed to comfortably seat five tall people.

The seating arrangements in the Omni were strict due to the limited space. My two sisters and I piled into the back seat and Mom was in the front passenger seat while Dad did most of the driving. My sister Shirley was squeezed in the middle of the back seat between me and our youngest sister, Kathy. Shirley devised a method of managing our limited space. She pointed to the seams in the seat's upholstery and declared the seams to be boundaries. "You can't cross this line," she would say, glaring at us with her most forbidding look. If we crossed a boundary, she would loudly remind us of the rules, poking us with her elbows to emphasize the point.

Mom, riding co-pilot in the front seat, would join in the fray. "Girls, stop whining!" she ordered, trying to break up the backseat brawl. Then she would pull out a package of crackers, trying to pacify us with snacks. Mom imposed a strict diet on these trips to save money and avoid eating in restaurants. Sandwiches, crackers, plain cookies and fruit were the standard fare. No drinks were allowed in the car because of the risk of spills and additional restroom breaks. I remember driving past fast-food restaurants and longing to order a burger and shake.

Eventually, my sisters and I were lulled to sleep by the movement of the car. One good thing that came out of the family trips was that we all learned to sleep in a moving vehicle. This is a wonderful habit for people like me who do a lot of traveling.

Once my sisters and I settled down into our seats, squeezed together like kittens trying to keep each other warm, Mom resumed her role as co-pilot.

This involved criticizing Dad's driving habits – "Slow down!"; "Watch that truck!"; "Light is red!" In addition to watching the road, Mom tracked the gas mileage in a notebook in the glove compartment. Tracking the gas use was a habit developed after the energy crisis in the 1970's which continues today.

Mom was also the chief navigator. Decades before smartphones and digital maps, we relied on maps and tour books. Getting to a new destination was not always easy; it involved reading signs, making correct turns and getting onto the highway going in the right direction. This was not easy when we were driving through a different state or in bad weather when signs were not visible.

Dad enjoyed driving and was generally patient with Mom's orders. He would get frustrated if we got lost since it meant losing time and wasting gas. If we ended up going in the wrong direction, he would lose his temper. "Darn it! We're supposed to be on the other side of the highway!"

"Watch your language!" Mom would reply sharply. Swearing was strictly forbidden in our family.

We were always looking for things to do on these long trips. Keeping busy helped us to forget that we were packed into the car for hours. We would listen to tapes, read books and play games such as Mad Libs.

One mode of entertainment was the CB radio, commonly used by truck drivers. After the song *Convoy* by C.W. McCall was released, people started putting CB radios in their cars. Dad liked electronic gadgets so he installed a CB radio in the car. Mom was skeptical about the CB, worried about the strange people we were talking to over the radio. My sisters and I thought the CB radio was like a game. We listened to Dad's conversations, helping him sign off with a "10-4 good buddy."

During one memorable trip to Florida, we were driving late into the evening. We didn't have a hotel reservation and every hotel we stopped at was full. Our cousins were traveling with us, crammed into the rear section of our Ford Country Squire station wagon. This was before current seatbelt and safety laws. Mom was driving and my aunt was in the front seat, playing around with the CB radio. All of a sudden, a voice boomed over the CB radio. "This is Moonshine callin' all good buddies on I-95 North in Florida." People talking on the radio used a call sign in place of their real names.

My aunt grabbed the CB handset along with the book that translated CB lingo into English and started conversing with Moonshine. A few minutes later, another voice squeaked through the speakers. "Hi y'all, this here's Sneakers." Both men were driving 18-wheel tractor trailer trucks, heading north to deliver their cargoes by Monday. Moonshine's truck was in front and Sneakers' truck was following behind. Mom pulled the station wagon up behind Sneakers' truck, creating a mini convoy.

As kids, we thought being part of a convoy was exciting. We got so riled up that we serenaded Sneakers and Moonshine with our version of the song *Convoy*. My aunt, who was bold and brash, adopted the call name "Big Cat." Of course, as kids, we were "the kittens." After a couple of hours, she had a rapport with Sneakers and Moonshine and it felt like they were our friends. The conversations helped the time to pass during our long drive.

When a sign for a "truck stop" appeared on the highway, the truck drivers decided it was time for us to meet in person. Moonshine's voice echoed through the car. "Hey there, Big Cat. How 'bout you and your kittens join us for a cuppa coffee?"

"Yeah, we'd like to meet you ladies up close 'n' personal," Sneakers chimed in.

My aunt grabbed the CB handset; we could see from the look on her face that she was about to accept the invitation. Mom tried to grab the handset from my aunt's hands. As Mom's left hand was holding onto the steering wheel and her right hand was wrestling with my aunt over the handset, the car veered to the right

"Are you crazy? Two women, alone with a bunch of kids, meeting strange truck drivers at a truck stop at night? I don't think so!" Mom shouted. She was always conservative and erred on the safe side.

My aunt looked disappointed, but she realized Mom was right. "Sorry Sneakers and Moonshine, but these cats need to keep on truckin' into the night," my aunt said into the CB handset.

"Aw, shucks, Big Cat; we was hopin' for a good night kiss," Sneakers replied.

My aunt held the handset close to her mouth and made the sound of kissing.

"All right, then it's 10-4 good buddies. We sure enjoyed your company. Moonshine out."

"Travel safely Big Cat 'n' kittens. Sneakers out."

All of us kids in the backseat were laughing and waving to the two truck drivers as they pulled their trucks off the highway. They blared their loud horns in response.

"That's it; one of our more interesting family trips," I said to Professor as I finished the story. I sat back in my seat and took a big breath, feeling strong emotions from my memories.

Professor was laughing. "That's a great story! I think you made it up."

"No, it's true. There are some things that you never forget."

"The interesting thing is that we now travel with sandwiches, crackers, homemade granola bars and bottles of water," Professor added.

"I know, but as a kid, I wanted fast food. It's funny and somewhat terrifying how you become more like your parents as you get older." I yawned, feeling sleepy after my hour of storytelling.

"You're right, we do become more like our parents," Professor said, thoughtfully. He squinted as he followed the signs for Iowa, our next destination.

15 LEWIS AND CLARK'S TRAIL

The scenery changed when we crossed the state line and entered Iowa. The world became bright green and fertile – alive with the sight and smells of busy farms. Trouble crawled out from under her sheet and pressed her nose against the mesh of the carrier, sniffing loudly to smell the sweet scent of clover and the pungent smell of cow manure.

"We're in Iowa, Trouble." I scratched her head through the mesh and she made a low, growling sound.

The growl usually means, "Right, but when do I get a snack and some freedom?"

"We'll be in Davenport soon and then you can get out of your carrier," I said to the cat.

Professor inhaled deeply. "Ah, the sweet smell of spring in Iowa."

We all perked up and stared out the window at the idyllic scene – lush green fields stretching across the horizon dotted with silos, barns and mature trees in full bloom. On many farms, a white farmhouse stood in the center of the field, surrounded by trees for protection against the hot summer sun and powerful winter winds. Some farms had wind turbines spinning slowly like giant pinwheels, generating electric power.

"I often dream about living on a farm with a traditional farmhouse set in the middle of a field. My dream farm would grow all kinds of fruits and vegetables and have chickens, horses, goats and sheep. I would make my own sheep cheese and goat yogurt and gather fresh eggs every morning," I said, envisioning the bucolic lifestyle.

"You have to get up at sunrise on a farm," Professor replied, sagely. "You don't like getting up early in the morning."

"That's true and farmers don't get many vacations; it's a difficult life." As a child, I attended a church with a congregation full of farmers. The farmers often looked tired and careworn, smelling like the animals in a barn. They rose early so they could finish their chores before coming to church. I let my farming idea slip away into memory, where it will remain a dream.

We arrived at a hotel in Davenport, Iowa where Trouble ran around the hotel room, checked out the view from the windows and then followed me around crying vociferously until I gave her some food. After dinner, she curled up in her fuzzy pink cat bed for a nap.

"You're such a good cat," I said, stroking the cat's silky fur. "You're an expert traveler."

"She really has become a good traveler." Professor was unpacking the bins from the luggage cart. "She remembers our routine and continues to learn new things along the way."

We ate a light dinner before reading our books and going to bed early. We had driven through four states since leaving Mom and Dad's house that morning and were exhausted.

Trouble woke up at sunrise, running around the hotel room and making all sorts of noise to let us know she was ready for breakfast. When I didn't get up right away, she sat on the bed next to my head, purring loudly in my ear.

After breakfast, we hurriedly packed up our food and belongings so we could drive to Sioux City, Iowa. After driving across Iowa on I-80, we pulled into the parking lot of the hotel in Sioux City. Trouble climbed the mesh of the pet carrier, trying to look out the car window. She clearly recognized this place from the sounds and smells of the Missouri River which runs next to the hotel.

Professor checked us into the hotel and we headed up to the fourth floor to a suite overlooking the river. After getting the cat settled, Professor and I went down to the paved path along the Missouri River. We had been looking forward to this moment all day. We strolled along the river, staying on the right side of the path so people on bikes could pass us. The path is lined with trees, bushes and flowers, creating a pleasant park for an evening walk or ride.

We sat silently on one of the benches on the riverbank watching the sunset. The sun was low on the horizon, casting long shadows across the muddy water. We watched the sky turning the full rainbow of colors, hinting at an eye-catching sunset. The Missouri River moves quickly and I watched several logs float past us at a surprising pace. Swifts were skimming the water, eating as many bugs as they could catch; a good thing since the mosquitoes were biting.

"We need to keep moving," I said, swatting at the mosquitoes. I always seem to attract them while they don't bother Professor. "I should have brought some mosquito repellent."

"I don't need mosquito repellent. I just need to stand next to you."

"Very funny!" I laughed while swatting at the large cloud of mosquitoes circling around my head.

As Professor and I continued walking up the path along the river, we saw several deer grazing in the grass. A rabbit was chewing on some green buds and a squirrel ran by carrying his evening snack. The birds were getting quieter, settling down as darkness closed in around the river.

Professor and I were reluctant to return to the hotel, still feeling cooped up after traveling for close to a week. However, there are no lights along the path so it would be easy to trip over a large tree root or wander off the path and slip into the moving water. So, we walked back to the hotel.

Back in the hotel room, I found Trouble sitting on the windowsill watching the river. She was very relaxed, enjoying the natural rhythms of this place. As I stroked the cat's fur, the sky turned into a swath of colors — magenta, red, orange and yellow. The colors were intense and then faded swiftly to gray and then black, as the last light of the sun disappeared.

The next day was a recovery day. Professor and I drove into the city to do some shopping leaving Trouble sitting contently on her perch overlooking the river. Our first stop was the supermarket. On the way, we passed the memorial to Sergeant Floyd, a member of Lewis and Clark's expedition team and the only person to die during the expedition. Professor enjoys discussing the Lewis and Clark expedition and keeps reminding me that we are following in their footsteps. There are many powerful reminders of their presence along our route through Iowa, South Dakota, Wyoming, and Montana.

As we passed the monument, Professor gave a mini-lecture on Lewis and Clark. "In May 1804, Lewis and Clark along with 31 other members of their team left St. Louis, traveling up the Missouri River. The expedition was assembled at the request of President Thomas Jefferson to explore the lands that America had just purchased from France for $15,000,000. The lands were mostly unexplored and wild, occupied by various Native American tribes."

"It's hard to imagine it now given all of the towns, cities, and farms along the Missouri River, but in 1804 the lands were totally wild and thriving with animals," Professor added.

We went to the local supermarket to stock up on supplies. I bought two packages of my favorite coffee from Sioux City roaster Jumpy Monkey — Sergeant Floyd's blend, a dark French roast with a bold flavor.

One of my lasting impressions of Iowa is that people are genuinely nice. In the spring, people are enthusiastic about getting outdoors. "It's time to mow the lawn," one of the employees said to me after asking me if I needed help with my shopping list.

At the cash register, the woman who rang up our purchases was also excited about the spring weather. "I'm going mushroom hunting with my brother this weekend," she said, brightly.

On our return trip to the hotel, Professor continued his musings on Lewis and Clark. He reminded me that we travel near many sites and memorials related to the expedition. The memorial to Sergeant Floyd in Sioux City is just one of many highway markers depicting various exploits from the expedition. Professor has been reading the journals written by the expedition leaders Captain Meriwether Lewis and Second Lieutenant William Clark. Full of day-to-day descriptions of life on the trail, some of the observations are fascinating. Clark was a keen observer of wildlife and identifies bears, wolves, birds, and the ever-present mosquitoes in their daily routine.

In the evening, Professor and I took another walk along the Missouri River. This time we walked more slowly, thinking about the next day. We had to be on the road early for the long drive through South Dakota.

"Tomorrow is a long day," I said, feeling dejected.

"It is, but we'll drive through the Badlands and we can stop at Wall Drug for ice cream," Professor said, optimistically.

We felt sad as we drove away from Sioux City the next morning. We looked forward to coming back at the end of the summer and taking more long walks on the Missouri River.

Our next destination was Rapid City, South Dakota. We stopped at our favorite rest stop in Chamberlain, South Dakota. The rest stop sits on top of a bluff overlooking the Missouri River. The rest stop has The Lewis & Clark I-90 Information Center, staffed by people who are always quick to smile and offer assistance. Outside the information center, standing on the edge of the bluff overlooking the river is an awe-inspiring statue, titled "Dignity." The gigantic statue of a Native American woman stands as a tribute to all Native American women. This statue is part of South Dakota's sculpture trail, described on the website, southdakotasculpturetrail.org, as "a free public art museum that stretches across the entire state with hundreds of world class sculptures to enjoy."

A sign near the visitor center has information about Toussaint Charbonneau, and his Shoshone wife, Sacagawea who acted as interpreters and guides for Lewis and Clark. Professor and I think the statue at the rest stop resembles Sacagawea and that is fitting given her importance to the exploration of the West. The rest stop is well-designed including large shade trees to keep Trouble cool. Professor pulled the car into a shaded parking space and opened the windows. I pulled back the sheet on top of Trouble's carrier and she ran close to the open window, lifting her face to greet the warm spring sun and sniffing loudly as the breeze blew over her whiskers. She greeted me with a short staccato of "meow, meow, meow," meaning "Is it time to get out and where is my treat?"

"Hello, my adorable cat," I said while sticking my hand into the carrier to stroke her silky fur. I was giving her extra hairball prevention gel and it was making her fur very soft and shiny.

Trouble responded with a loud persistent "yowl!" She was more interested in a snack than my attention. I gave her a tasty cat treat and then unpacked our lunch from the cooler – turkey sandwiches, fruit, yogurt, cottage cheese – again. At this point in the trip we were tired of sandwiches, but this is what works on a long drive across the country.

The rest stop has concrete benches which are sheltered from the sun and wind, both of which can be intense on the bluff. Leaving the car window open and Trouble with her face pressed against the mesh of her carrier, Professor and I settled on a nearby picnic bench.

"It's good to have a break from driving. This is my favorite rest stop for lunch." Professor chewed his sandwich thoughtfully. "It's a great place to think about the history of Lewis and Clark."

"It's always very pleasant to stop here and recover from driving," I replied quickly, hoping to avoid another lecture. "People are nice, too."

I stood up to throw away some trash in the nearby garbage can and saw a flash of white fur. "Did you see something?" I asked Professor, while looking behind the trash can.

"No, I didn't see anything. What did you see?" Professor had a faraway look, thinking about Lewis and Clark's travels, while he was eating a chocolate chip cookie.

"I thought I saw a cat," I replied. "I did! I did!" Professor giggled as I realized I sounded like a famous cartoon character.

I walked behind the picnic shelter and saw a paper plate, half full of dry cat food. Behind the plate, a small cat with short, white fur was hiding in the bushes, peering at me with curiosity.

"Come here, little cat," I called to her. She ran into the bushes, obviously not trusting strange humans.

I was drawn to the sweet face and worried about the cat's safety. I knelt down and put my hand out. The cat sniffed my hand and then shrank back into the bushes. I imagined that this cat belonged to nice people. They put the cat in their RV while they traveled across the country. When they got to this rest stop, they opened the door of the RV, forgetting to watch for the cat because they were weary from driving. The cat, tired of driving, was sitting by the door, waiting to get out. As the people opened the door, a motorcycle drove by. The loud noise scared the cat who jumped out of the RV and ran into the nearby wooded area. No amount of calling by the people would bring the cat out of the hiding place. They eventually gave up and continued with their travels.

The cat was not wearing a collar so when the nice ladies at the rest stop found her, they didn't know who to contact. They fed the cat and did their best to care for her.

"You have a very active imagination. Most likely she's just a feral cat," Professor said, after listening to my explanation.

"You're probably right, but I feel sorry for the little cat," I said, glancing at the bushes.

"Well, we have our own cat to worry about. We need to get Trouble to Montana safely."

Professor was right so I cleaned up the remains of our lunch and went back to the car to check on Trouble. The first thing I did was check the zipper on the end of the carrier to make sure it was secure. I didn't want Trouble to end up as a stray cat at a rest stop. She licked my fingers after eating a treat.

"You're such a good cat," I said while scratching behind her ears. "We'll take good care of you; don't worry. You have to be around for a long time." I couldn't imagine life without my cat.

We left the Chamberlain rest stop and continued on our trip. As promised, Professor pulled off at Wall Drug Store after seeing the hand-painted signs for miles before the exit. Wall Drug Store was started by the Hustead family in the 1930's. Now it's a small Western town with shopping, restaurants and entertainment for weary travelers.

After Wall Drug, we drove through Badlands National Park, which reminds me of pictures of the moon taken by astronauts. Early in the evening, we pulled into the parking lot of a Rapid City, South Dakota hotel. The hotel was full of tourists going to Mt. Rushmore and the Crazy Horse Monument.

As we settled into our room, Professor was reading the National Park Service website and offered a lecture on the Badlands. "Badlands National Park is a unique geologic wonderland filled with colors and contrasts. Badlands started as a national monument in 1929 and became a national park in 1978. The area has been inhabited for thousands of years with the ancestors of the Lakota people who have been hunting in the area for millennia. The Lakota people probably gave the area its name; they called this place 'mako sica' or 'land bad.' The name is appropriate given its harsh environment dominated by rugged terrain, extreme heat and cold, and arid soil."

Professor paused to see if I was listening. I nodded as he continued, "The unusual geology has been defined by two processes: deposition and erosion. Sedimentary rock in the area was formed from cemented sands, silt, and clay over the last 75 million years as the area transitioned from open sea, tropical jungle, to woodland environments. Episodic volcanic eruptions deposited vast quantities of ash over the area. About 500,000 years ago, rivers and streams carved up the rock and soils into the fantastic shapes and bands of color that visitors see in Badlands National Park today."

We got the cat settled and tried to relax. Trouble ran around the room playing with her toys and listening to kids out in the hallway as they ran to the aquatic center in the hotel. Professor studied the map and sighed. We would be driving through Wyoming the next day, finally getting into the wide-open spaces that we crave when we are on the East coast.

16 THE OLD WEST

As I woke up, I reached for my phone on the bedside table to turn off the music that plays when the alarm goes off. The song was *Take Me Home, Country Roads*, by John Denver, an appropriate theme song for this trip. I was only half awake and Professor was still sound asleep. Trouble's fuzzy cat bed, sitting on the end of our bed, was empty. I recalled that we were in South Dakota, with two more days of driving before we arrived in Bozeman.

Trouble jumped up next to my head, purring loudly in my ear and licking my face. She is a sweet, loving cat, but I also know that she does this to get me out of bed as soon as possible. I heard her stomach growling so I knew she was hungry for breakfast. We were scheduled for an early start, so I got up to feed the cat, careful to not wake Professor. Trouble deserved to be pampered.

After Trouble ate her breakfast, Professor and I went to the hotel lobby to grab a quick breakfast. We were both cranky and short-tempered, yelling at each other for no reason. We were worn out from traveling day after day and not sleeping well in hotel rooms. When we returned to our room and started packing up our belongings and supplies, the cat was very restless. She kept looking for a place to hide – jumping on top of the furniture, countertops and cabinets, and trying to crawl behind the television and under the bed. The cat was also tired of traveling. Thankfully, this hotel room did not have any good cat hiding spaces.

An hour later, we were in the car, sitting in the same places as the day before, and the day before... and the day before.

As we drove through South Dakota and into Wyoming, Professor slowed the car down, looking for Devil's Tower, a giant hexagonal rock which juts up against the horizon. It's a National Monument because of its rarity.

Professor offered a history lesson on Devil's Tower, which spikes up out of the prairie west of the Black Hills. "The tower is actually the remnants of an ancient geologic formation developed millions of years ago. It is formed of a rare igneous rock, phonolite porphyry, and is the largest example of columnar jointing in the world. Apparently, other rocks and soils surrounding the tower eroded away over time exposing the feature. The rock is still considered a sacred place by local Native American tribes."

We visited Devil's Tower on one of our trips out West with Mom and Dad. I remembered being in awe at the rock climbers near the top of Devil's Tower.

"The tower is also a world-renowned rock climbing venue as the 1,267-foot high tower has hundreds of vertical cracks between the various hexagonal columnar rock formations. These cracks, varying in size, allow rock climbers of many skill levels to ascend the tower," Professor added.

The scenery changed as we entered Wyoming. Driving through Wyoming, we finally saw the Rocky Mountain range and experienced the amazing wide-open spaces. The Rocky Mountains seemingly appear out of thin air when driving west through Wyoming. It is hard to describe their majesty, but each time we see them we are mesmerized. The Rocky Mountains form a vast collection of different mountain ranges, some 100 of them, that stretch about 3,000 miles from New Mexico to Western Canada. In some places they are up to 300 miles wide and up to 14,000 feet high. The different mountain ranges are composed of many types of rock ranging from limestone to granite lending a unique character to each separate range that makes each distinct yet still part of a larger colony.

We sat silently, watching the scenery, as the car went up and down the hills and wound around sharp curves. Our car was the only vehicle on the road. As we climbed in elevation, Trouble started howling – a loud, plaintive, high-pitched noise that pierced the silence inside the car.

"You need to pull the car off the road," I said to Professor, taking in a deep breath through my nose. "I don't smell anything, but it sounds like Trouble has used her box."

"Where do you expect me to pull the car off the road?" Professor responded sharply, weary of traveling and unexpected stops. "There are no rest stops out here."

I looked outside the car – all I could see were open fields, mountains, and an occasional lake. Driving west on I-90, the first range encountered in the Rocky Mountains is the Big Horn Range. The range is stunning as the peaks rise suddenly out of the high plains landscape with elevations over 13,000 feet. It almost feels as if you are going to drive into a wall on I-90 when the highway veers northwest and skirts the eastern side of the Big Horn Range. In the spring, the whole range is snow covered and they shimmer like a mirage in the sunshine and blue sky.

Every so often, I saw a couple of horses or a herd of cattle with tiny calves standing close to their mothers. There were no rest stops, no places to pull the car off the road and no signs of civilization.

"Pull off anywhere," I replied, wearily. Trouble was wailing loudly and it was difficult to think clearly.

Professor finally pulled the car off the highway into a scenic viewpoint. I checked on Trouble and gave her a treat as she purred contentedly. The litter box was clean.

"Is her box dirty?" Professor was standing and stretching his back and shoulders which were cramped from driving. He insists on doing most of the driving even though I am a good driver.

"No."

"Then what's the matter with our cat?"

"I guess her ears must be bothering her with the change in elevation. I think she did this last year." I didn't say anything more to Professor, but I believe our cat learns to yowl loudly knowing that when she does, the car stops and she gets a treat. I put some of Trouble's hairball prevention gel on my finger and she licked it greedily. I hoped this would help open up her ears. We got back into the car and continued on the highway. The sky was a clear, bright blue and as the car crested a hill, we felt like we could see to the ends of the Earth.

We arrived at our hotel in Buffalo, Wyoming in the early afternoon. The town was very quiet and reminiscent of an earlier era. It was easy to picture a time when the roads were made from dirt and people rode their horses when they needed to get somewhere.

Trouble seemed to recognize the hotel; we stayed in the same room last year. I wondered how well they clean these hotel rooms and whether she could still smell her scent. After eating her dinner, she hopped onto the bed and rolled around on the snow-white quilt.

Then Trouble jumped from the bed to the window and settled into the sunniest spot. I stood behind her, scratching behind her ears. She pressed her head into my hand, purring contentedly as we both started to relax. We looked out the window at a small farm with a lush green field, a babbling brook and a wooden slat fence. Two horses, one white, one dark brown, were grazing in the fields. Mountain peaks stretched across the horizon, stark against the brilliant blue sky. Trouble and I both sighed as we relished in this scene of the West.

A young girl walked out into the field and started training the brown horse. She patiently guided the horse through the exercises, gently bringing him back on track when he stubbornly moved in a different direction. I was fascinated with the training session and kept watching while Professor napped and Trouble snoozed in the sun.

Later, while Professor and I ate dinner, we reminisced about another trip to Wyoming.

On one of our trips with Mom and Dad, we drove to Sheridan, Wyoming.

We sat in our usual positions with Professor driving the four-door sedan and Dad riding co-pilot in the front passenger seat. Mom and I sat silently in the back seat, our knuckles gripping the door handles. Professor had decided to take the scenic route to Sheridan. We drove on Alternate U.S. Highway 14 – a highway carved into the mountainside, with blind curves, hairpin switchbacks and steep inclines and declines. Many sections of the road did not have a guardrail. As Professor drove the car through the dangerous curves in the road, we looked out the car windows, over the edge of cliffs to the valley floor thousands of feet below us. Mom and I were petrified. We did our best to stay silent so Professor could concentrate on driving the steep winding road.

Dad enjoyed himself. As the car drove dangerously close to the edge of cliffs that were not protected by guardrails he cheered, "Whoopee – this is great!" Dad always enjoyed a good roller coaster ride and driving this highway had a similar effect.

Eventually, we arrived in Sheridan. After getting settled into the historic Sheridan Inn hotel, established in 1893 and known as the "Home of Buffalo Bill," we started to recover from the harrowing car ride. We ate a satisfying dinner in the dining room and then walked around, absorbing the history that is ingrained into the walls of the hotel. We admired the well-kept, dark wood of the antique bar. The bartender was chatty and Mom struck up a conversation.

"Are you going to the parade tomorrow?" the bartender asked.

"What parade?" we asked in unison.

"The rodeo parade goes right through town. It's a big event; you shouldn't miss it." The bartender turned away to help another customer. We all agreed to go to the parade and went to bed with anticipation of the event.

The next morning, we went to the Silver Spur Cafe for breakfast. A local icon, this cozy cafe serves a hearty Western-style breakfast, fit for a busy cowboy or hungry travelers. Mom quickly assimilated into the family style dining room and soon knew all of the people sitting at our table. The pancakes were as big as my plate and I needed extra coffee to overcome the sleepy feeling from eating a big meal.

After breakfast, we followed the crowd and found a space near the curb so we would have a good view of the festivities. We were excited since we had not planned to see the parade and felt fortunate for our good timing. We saw lots of horses in the parade with glossy coats shining in the bright summer sunlight and riders dressed in classic Western-style clothing, sitting straight and tall in their saddles. We sensed their pride in the heritage and traditions being celebrated on that day.

Our favorite part of the parade was the Native American floats. Standing on large flatbed trailers, groups of Native Americans dressed in traditional ceremonial regalia were dancing to the beat of the drums. We took many photos, but they did not capture the splendor of the clothing, jewelry and headdresses. Sheridan hosts the First Peoples' Pow Wow every summer so this is an annual tradition.

"Remember how Dad got lost?" Professor interrupted me as I was reminiscing about the Sheridan rodeo parade. We were sitting on a bench next to our hotel in Buffalo, watching the birds fly around the stream outside our hotel.

"Of course," I said while nodding my head. "Dad always wanders away to take a photo and forgets to tell us where he is going."

After the Sheridan rodeo parade, Professor, Mom and I got up from our seats on the curb and turned to walk back to our hotel. We stepped carefully around the piles of horse manure littering the street. It was time to move on to our next destination.

"Where's Dad?" Mom asked, turning to look in every direction. Professor and I started looking around the crowded street; we did not see Dad anywhere.

"Dad!" I shouted. His habit of disappearing was very annoying when we were traveling and on a tight schedule. This was long before we all had cellphones, so our only option was to look for him.

We walked around town asking people if they had seen a tall, bald man wearing a plaid flannel shirt and a large camera around his neck. No one had seen Dad. Next, we went back to the hotel, but he wasn't there. By this point we were panicking. "Where could he have gone?" Mom cried, taking a tissue out of her pocket to wipe tears off her face.

"Don't worry, Mother; we will find him. You know he always wanders off." Professor patted Mom's shoulder reassuringly.

"This is so frustrating!" I yelled. The train was going through town and I raised my voice to be heard over the noise.

We all looked in the direction of the loud train. As the last car of the train went by, we had a clear view of the other side of the tracks. Dad was standing there, happily waving at us as if he was supposed to be there and there was no reason for concern. He had crossed the tracks to get a photo and then got stuck on the other side of the train.

"We've been looking for you for over an hour! What were you doing over there?" Mom was angry and frustrated. She waved her hand in the direction of the train tracks.

"I wanted to get a picture of the train station," Dad said, oblivious to the fact that he had caused tremendous worry. This was not the first time that Dad had wandered away, leaving us frantically searching for him. There was no doubt that it would not be the last time.

Professor and I finished talking about our adventures with Mom and Dad and returned to our hotel room in Buffalo. We went to bed early feeling excited. Tomorrow we would arrive at our destination – Bozeman, Montana.

17 SICK CAT IN BOZEMAN

After 10 days of traveling between Florida and Montana, we finally arrived in Bozeman, Montana. Professor pulled our car into the parking space in front of our condo unit and we both exhaled deeply, relieved to be at our destination. We were exhausted after traveling across the country but also excited to be at our second home. It was early spring – the trees were budding, the birds were noisy with mating calls and the air was brisk. People were packing away their heavy winter clothes and planning their summer camping trips.

Bozeman has a long history related to the mountains. John Bozeman, a frontiersman from Georgia who led wagon trains west to the gold fields in the Montana Territory, founded the town in 1864. The area served as a supply hub for prospectors who hoped to find their fortune.

Today Bozeman is a small city with a vibrant culture fueled by energy from Montana State University (MSU). The mountain ranges surrounding the city offer limitless opportunities for outdoor activities. In the summer, the city bustles with farmers' markets, art walks, concerts and theater productions.

We looked forward to all of these activities while we unpacked our car. Professor carried Trouble and her carrier into the condo. He returned to the car to start unpacking all of the bins while I took care of the cat. Trouble was clawing the mesh on the side of the carrier and yowling. She smelled her scent in the condo and she was ready to get settled. I looked carefully at the cat. I knew she was weary from traveling; we all were. It's stressful for her to be in the car for many hours and I worried about her health every day. She sensed that she was about to be free, looked up at me and blinked – a cat's way of smiling. I felt the strain of traveling drain out of my body. I laughed and patted Trouble's head, certain that she was happy to be with her family in her second home.

I unzipped the carrier and Trouble leaped out and ran up the stairs. I followed her to make sure she was okay and to check on the condition of our condo. I found her in the guest bedroom, sitting in the front window. From this window, she has a view of the Bridger Mountains, a sub-range of the Rocky Mountains in southwestern Montana, and the condo community parking lot. During our stay, she will sit in this window for hours, watching the neighbors coming and going during the day.

Next, Trouble jumped down from the window and raced down the stairs. Our house in Florida does not have stairs, so running up and down the stairs is a treat for Trouble. Over the course of the summer, she builds muscle and loses fat, becoming what Professor calls "a lean mean cat machine."

I followed the cat into the kitchen where she was sitting on a chair with a thick pad on the seat. Trouble has a knack for finding the softest spots in any room – in a house, condo or hotel room. From that chair, she could see out the sliding glass door and watch the birds in the trees in the backyard. Soon the neighbor's cats would sense our presence and push their faces against the glass door. Trouble is not friendly to other cats; she will hiss and puff out her tail to let them know that this condo is her territory.

One enjoyable experience of traveling with the cat is watching her learn new things. Trouble is adaptable – learning quickly and adopting new habits. She even invents new games and trains us to play along. She taught us to play soccer with her favorite yellow ball. She pushes the ball, I push it back and then she swats it like she is trying to score a goal. Traveling with my cat has led me to believe animals are intelligent in ways we do not fully understand.

During our first year in Bozeman, Trouble had to learn many new things. One challenge was getting onto the window sills. She enjoys siting in a sunny window and watching the activity outside the window. The condo has several big windows and the window sills are twice as high as the window sills in our house in Florida. It took some practice for Trouble to learn to jump onto the condo windowsills. Initially, she would sit on the furniture near the window then jump from the furniture to the windowsill, barely making it. Next, she started jumping up from the floor, using her back legs to scramble up the wall. Finally, she learned to gracefully leap from the floor to the windowsill in one smooth motion. Now, she automatically leaps up onto the windowsill, even after being away for eight months.

As I was unpacking bins in the kitchen, Trouble sat serenely, perfectly balanced on the windowsill, watching Professor unload the bins from the car. Trouble pushed her face closer to the window; she saw the two Siamese cats who live in a condo on the other side of the parking lot. They were licking their paws after eating breakfast and didn't seem to be aware of Trouble's presence.

Trouble remembers other habits and training from one year to the next.

For example, she always rushes to the front door when we are opening it and sits right behind the door. The heavy door could injure her, so Professor trained Trouble to jump on the step behind the door. As he opens the front door, he says, "On step, kitty; on the step!" Trouble jumps up on the step, avoiding the door and waiting patiently for us to come in.

The cat mirrors our own experience. Traveling, exploring new places and having diverse experiences broadens our minds and enriches our spirits. We enjoy a sense of adventure when traveling to a new place and a pleasant routine when rediscovering a favorite place.

Things didn't go as smoothly during our first summer in Bozeman. Professor only allowed six days for our drive across the country. We spent an average of eight hours in the car – every day. We all felt stressed and Trouble didn't eat much food or drink enough water.

When we arrived in Bozeman that first year, we were all exhausted. I took naps every day, trying to recover from the trip and adjust to the elevation. Trouble slept all night and most of the day, often curling up next to me when I was sleeping. I felt guilty about putting my cat through so much stress so I bought her a new toy – a cat perch which I put next to the window. Then I went to the local pet store looking for some delicious cat treats.

"Try this one," the salesperson said, handing me a bag of treats with a picture of an adorable kitten on the front. "We just got these in."

"My cat can't have any treats that will make her constipated." I was squinting to read the fine print on the list of package ingredients. "She normally has some issues with constipation. The wrong food could make it worse," I added.

"Oh, no problem! These treats are good for constipation," she said cheerily, pushing a second package into my hands.

I wanted Trouble to be content and relaxed – like the sweet kitten pictured on the front of the package of treats. The sales pitch worked and I bought two packages. Trouble devoured the treats. I normally limit her to two to three treats per day, but she gobbled up the treats and looked at me with pleading eyes. Before I realized it, she had eaten 10 treats.

"Are you sure Trouble should be eating so many of those treats?" Professor scowled as the cat continued to chew the treats.

"The salesperson said they would help her constipation," I replied defensively, letting Trouble eat another treat out of my hand.

"Okay." Professor took off his glasses to read the tiny print with the list of ingredients on the package of treats. "These treats have brown rice in them. Brown rice can be constipating."

"Well, hopefully the treats will digest well." I looked at Trouble who was cleaning her paws. She seemed fine, but I felt the seeds of worry start to grow in my mind.

The next day, Trouble seemed fine. She ate a little less food for breakfast than normal, but she seemed to have more energy. I kept checking her litter box. She hadn't pooped for a couple days; this was overdue.

The second day after eating the treats, Trouble stopped eating. She normally devours her food. Instead, she looked at the bowl of food and walked away. She was listless and avoided her litter box.

By the afternoon, we were sitting in the veterinarian's office. "She's severely constipated," the doctor said. "We can give her a kitty enema. If it works quickly, she can go home today. Otherwise, she will have to stay overnight."

"Overnight?" I was holding Trouble while the doctor gave us the prognosis. I had never been to this animal hospital before; I didn't know these people. How could I leave my cat here overnight? Trouble had never stayed in a vet's office for more than a few hours. I worried about her being stressed and lonely. Also, I was not used to sleeping without my cat next to me.

Professor patted me gently on the shoulder; a reminder that I needed to contain my anxiety. Professor and the doctor were talking about the next steps. I didn't hear most of it; I was still distraught over leaving my cat in the hands of a veterinarian who I had never met before. Trouble and I were used to our veterinarian in Florida, who has treated her since we took her into our household.

"Don't worry; we'll take good care of Trouble." The vet's assistant was carrying Trouble into the back room.

Professor and I went home and waited for the vet to call. He sat doing work on his computer while I moved anxiously about the house, going from one task to the next. I kept thinking that I heard the bell on Trouble's collar and then looked around only to realize that she was not in the house.

"You are too attached to the cat." Professor was watching me dust the living room for the third time.

"Maybe, but she's my little buddy. I miss her when she's not here."

"She'll be okay. She might even be home tonight," he said in an overly optimistic tone usually reserved for his students.

The vet called a short time later. She had given Trouble an enema, but it had only worked a little bit. They would give her another one and keep her overnight for observation.

I didn't sleep well that night. I tossed and turned, worrying about Trouble and expecting to see her sleeping at the end of the bed. When I didn't see her, I panicked before realizing that she was still in the veterinarian's office.

The vet called early the next morning. The enema had worked and Trouble was eating breakfast. We could pick her up at any time.

We sat in the waiting room at the vet's office for half an hour, waiting for the doctor to talk to us about Trouble's status. I tried to meditate on the tropical fish swimming in the large tank. Instead, I found myself feeling sad for the fish who were cooped up in the small tank, destined for a life of swimming around in circles.

I looked at the pet owners sitting on the opposite side of the room. An elderly lady sat very still, anxiously waiting for the vet assistant to bring her pet out. When they finally brought the cat to her, the woman's face lit up with a wide smile. Pets bring so much joy to their owners.

Next to the elderly lady, a young man sat looking at his smartphone and holding the leash for a portly Corgi. While the man was focused on the phone, the Corgi walked across the room to sniff my shoes. The man looked up. "Oh, sorry," he said, reeling the dog back in on the leash. The man stared at his phone again, the dog walked across the room to sniff my leg and the man reeled the dog in again. This continued for half an hour.

Finally, the technician brought Trouble out in her small carrier. "Come on, Trouble; let's get you home," I said, grabbing the carrier and walking quickly to the door. I was anxious to get out of the noisy waiting room.

Professor was standing at the front desk paying the bill. "Did you say $500?" He was talking loudly, shocked at the amount.

The receptionist nodded her head in an uncaring fashion. Trips to the veterinarian are always expensive.

Trouble perked up once we got her home. She ate a lot of food for dinner and slept all night in her usual spot at the end of the bed. The next morning, she was up on the windowsill watching the activity in the parking lot.

Thankfully, we had the opportunity to learn from this mistake. I researched cat food and learned to make healthy choices, avoiding the unhealthy ingredients that are put into many pet foods. Since we switched to higher quality cat food, Trouble has not had a problem with severe constipation.

This summer, we were looking forward to relaxing and enjoying all that Montana has to offer during the brief summer season. We also hoped that Professor, Trouble and I would enjoy good health during our adventures.

18 GRIZZLY BEARS

In Montana, we enjoy getting out into the mountains, taking time to walk slowly, enjoying everything that Mother Nature has to offer – the seasonal changes in the trees, the sounds of birds, the variety of wildlife, colorful flowers and sparkling lakes. The scenery on the trails changes from year to year, impacted by the weather, climate change and wildlife activity. Occasionally, we encounter large wildlife such as bears.

We left the condo early one July morning. Trouble ate her breakfast and then followed me to the front door, with a soft "Mewl," which means, "Why are you disrupting our morning routine?"

"We'll be back later, Trouble," I said, patting her on the head. "Be a good cat," I added, hopefully. Even though she was 12-years-old, she could still be rambunctious. Trouble jumped on her favorite chair and peered out the window at us as we got into our car.

Arriving at the parking lot for the trail, we walked up to the sign board near the trailhead to read the notices from the US Forest Service. Reading the notices is important for safety reasons. Last year there was a notice telling hikers to avoid a certain section of the trail because a bear was feeding on a moose carcass.

I noticed a new sign which read, "Notice to Hunters – Grizzly Bears in the Area…" I didn't read any further.

"Grizzly bears!" I exclaimed. "Grizzly bears are not supposed to be in this area."

Professor was staring at the notice, looking bewildered. He hikes regularly with a group of avid hikers and no one had mentioned grizzly bears being in the area. Word usually gets around about such things. "Maybe it's just precautionary. Grizzly bears are continuing to spread across areas of the state. It's probably just a matter of time before a grizzly bear moves into this area." Professor spoke slowly. He won't admit it, but he's afraid of bears.

"Right, that would make sense. We haven't heard anything about grizzly bears in this area. Surely it would be in the news if there was even one grizzly." I was confident that if anyone had seen a grizzly bear, it would have been reported in the local news.

Grizzly bears, often called "grizzlies," are a source of controversy in Montana. Grizzlies once roamed all over the West. As people moved into these areas, they killed the bears to protect themselves and their property. By the 1970's, only a few grizzlies remained, mostly in Glacier and Yellowstone National Parks and remote areas in the Rocky Mountains. In 1975, grizzlies were classified as an endangered species, protected under federal laws.

In 2017, the population in the Greater Yellowstone Ecosystem was removed from the list as the studies indicated that population had recovered. This was great news for the grizzly bears and the biologists who worked hard to bring back the population. However, as the number of bears has increased, the grizzlies have been on the move, spreading across the state and going back into their historic territory. The challenge is that people and other animals, including domestic livestock, now live in that territory.

In the March-April 2018 issue of *Montana Outdoors* published by Montana Fish Wildlife & Parks, the state agency responsible for managing these issues, the cover shows a photo of a grizzly bear with the headline "Can we co-exist? – Resolving conflicts in Montana's growing grizzly country." The article discussed the increasing number of conflicts with grizzly bears, resulting in harm to bears, cattle and sometimes people. The incidents are rare, but they always make headlines in the local news, creating the impression that grizzly bears are attacking livestock and property all over the state. The article details the steps that state wildlife officials are taking to work with local communities to help prevent such conflicts.

Now that the grizzly population is recovering, there are concerns about keeping the bears safe and healthy. Bears have been hit by cars, died after eating pesticide left open in garages, removed or euthanized after eating pet food and birdseed in backyards and shot by landowners after killing livestock.

Although rare, people have been attacked by grizzly bears. These encounters usually occur when the person surprises the bear and more often when the bear is a female protecting cubs. A mother bear will resort to violence to protect her offspring. As such, many people believe they should be able to hunt grizzly bears. Some advocate that hunted bears will be afraid of humans and more likely to avoid populated areas. Other people believe the grizzlies should be left alone to continue to expand their population. Although they no longer meet the definition of an endangered species, there are still very few bears compared to the number that existed when Lewis and Clark tracked through the state in 1805.

Living in Montana means learning to co-exist with wildlife. We do our best to follow the rules for hiking in bear country – not hiking alone, making noise by talking and clapping, trying not to drop food on or near the trail, and carrying bear spray. A fed bear will associate people with food and keep returning to the same place. These bears often end up being euthanized as a potential danger to humans.

Professor and I carry cans of bear spray, but we have never used it. Although we have seen many black bears, they either ran in the other direction or made enough noise to let us know that we needed to move out of their territory.

At the beginning of the summer, I practiced using the bear spray which is in a tall red canister. I pressed the trigger to deploy the spray – a pepper oil mixture which creates a cloud that usually stops a bear in its tracks, giving the humans a chance to back away slowly. The spray is powerful so when my finger pressed the trigger, I felt a kickback as the spray shot forcefully out of the can.

Professor and I finished reading the grizzly bear warning sign at the trailhead and continued up the trail. We planned to hike eight miles and be back to our condo after lunch. By 4 p.m. I would be in my favorite chair, having a well-deserved nap with Trouble sitting on my lap. As we started walking up the trail, we reminisced about our grizzly bear encounters. Professor's usual calm demeanor changes when he is hiking in bear country. He suffers from what I call "severe bear anxiety." I believe this goes back to our experience with grizzly bears while camping in Yosemite.

On a trip to Yosemite National Park, we stayed at a campground in the park in a platform tent. Professor checked us in at the office in the campground while I waited in the car. He returned to the car visibly distraught. While waiting in line, he watched videos of grizzly bears tearing the doors off a car. The Yosemite bears have learned that cars often have food in them. A bear's nose is so powerful that it can smell food from miles away. Bears will also return to a site after finding food in that location.

In order to prevent the Yosemite grizzlies from causing injuries and property damage, the campground rules were very strict. All snacks and toiletries, including lotions and toothpaste, had to be locked in a metal, bear-proof box. All trash had to be placed in a bear-proof trash can. Professor was spooked by the videos and so we carefully followed every rule. Each night before we went to bed, we scoured our rental car to make sure it was clear of anything that could attract a bear. We carefully put all of our snacks and toiletries into our metal locker before going to bed.

One night, I couldn't sleep because there was a lot of noise in the campground. The tents were very close together, so we could hear everything. I could also hear gunshots as the Park Rangers fired guns to scare bears away from the campground. Around 2 a.m., I heard a ranger talking loudly to the two elderly ladies staying in the tent behind us.

"Do you have a blue car, with this license plate number?" He rattled off the number.

I heard the ladies scrambling around in the tent, trying to get dressed in the pitch-black darkness.

"Yes, is there a problem, Ranger?" One of the ladies spoke softly, as if she was afraid of the answer to her question.

"There was a banana in the car and a bear broke into the car. I need you to come and identify the car and fill out a report." The Ranger spoke calmly, as if this was an everyday occurrence.

The women sounded very upset and I heard lots of scraping and stomping noises as they finished getting dressed and went with the Ranger to look at the damage to their car. I didn't hear them come back until after sunrise. Professor and I didn't get any more sleep that night.

Since that time, we have seen quite a few bears in our travels. Most of the bears have been small black bears who usually turn and run in the other direction when they smell us. We once thought we saw a grizzly bear while walking on the Bear Basin Trail in Big Sky, Montana, a ski resort. We turned to look in the direction of a deep growl and saw a large brown bear sitting under a near-by tree. It may have been a grizzly bear or a cinnamon brown black bear. We didn't take the time to look more closely. There are specific identifying characteristics for grizzly bears – teddy bear ears, a large hump on the back and a pointed snout. Professor was certain it was a grizzly bear. We backed away slowly, holding our hiking poles up in the air to make ourselves look bigger and taking out our bear spray. My heart was pounding so loud that I could barely hear Professor talking. I'm not sure what he was saying, but it was probably related to his bear anxiety.

We spoke quietly to the bear. "Hello, Mr. Bear, we are not going to hurt you so please just let us keep going on our way." It sounds silly, but talking quietly soothes our cat, so we figured it wouldn't do any harm.

I felt calm, but I sensed Professor was on the verge of panicking. "Walk slowly," I reminded him. I knew he was visualizing the images of Yosemite grizzly bears destroying cars and thinking about what this powerful bear might do to us if he was upset by our presence.

"No need to panic," I reminded both Professor and the bear. We continued to back slowly down the trail until we felt we reached a safe distance from the bear who never moved and didn't make any more noise. I imagined him snoring peacefully in the shade having nightmares about annoying hikers.

Later, we were sitting at the Hungry Moose Cafe in the Big Sky Town Center, drinking coffee and sharing a sandwich. Professor was still showing signs of severe bear anxiety; he had been afraid that the bear would charge us.

"We followed all of the rules." I was strangely calm. I worry about just about everything in life, but getting attacked by a bear is not something that concerns me. We follow the accepted rules and have not had a problem.

However, I have heard many stories about people who dismiss the rules, risking their lives. One of our friends told us about an incident in Yellowstone National Park. He and his family were driving through the park when they were stopped by an animal jam. The Park Rangers were corralling people, watching a grizzly bear sow and her two cubs. The three bears started walking toward the line of cars parked by the side of the road and then stopped next to a car.

Suddenly, a woman jumped out of a car and unfolded a tripod right next to the bears. The woman placed a camera on top of the tripod and started taking photos of the bears.

The Rangers were screaming "Get back in the car!" The woman continued taking photos, oblivious to the warning. Eventually, the bears moved on and the photographer received a citation for harassing wildlife and endangering people and property.

"So, even though the bears had every opportunity to attack a person, they just went on their way." I finished my story as Professor chewed his sandwich thoughtfully.

I reminded Professor about how we have had many incidents during our years of hiking, including being accosted by aggressive dogs, but problems with bears is not one of them. We have seen or heard at least a dozen bears in our travels, most of them black bears and have never had an issue.

We finished our hike and returned to our home in the city, feeling refreshed and less worried about the grizzly bear sign. Trouble greeted us at the door, yawning and stretching as if she had just awakened from a nap. However, it was clear from the evidence that she had been active all day:

-Cat paw marks on top of the stove and the refrigerator;

-Smudges on the sliding glass door where she pressed her nose to stare at the birds in the yard;

-Flakes of cardboard from her scratch pad, strewn about the living room;

-Poo on the rug near her box;

-Holes in the back of the faux leather chair, which she climbs like a tree;

-Sheets bunched up on the bed where she snuggled during her nap.

"I guess you had an active day, Trouble," I said while putting food in her dish. "And people wonder why your name is Trouble."

The next day we rode our bikes to the local U.S. Forest Service Office in Bozeman. The Ranger at the front desk said the grizzly bear sign was "precautionary" and there were "no confirmed sightings of grizzly bears" in the area.

"So, you can hike without worrying about grizzlies," I said to Professor as we rode our bikes back to our condo.

"They will be in this area one of these days; it's a matter of time," he replied.

19 GRANNY LOST IN BEEHIVE BASIN

When the temperatures rise in Bozeman, we like to drive up to Big Sky which is at a higher elevation and often 10 degrees cooler than the city. On this day, we planned to hike the Beehive Basin trail outside of Big Sky, Montana, a scenic day hike in the Rocky Mountains. Beehive Basin hiking trail starts on the outskirts of the Big Sky ski resort and is located amongst million-dollar homes with spectacular views of Lone Peak Mountain. We left Trouble sprawled on the floor of our condo which is cool from the damp air in the crawl space below the condo. By the afternoon, she would be lying by the sliding glass door stretched across a patch of sun.

On our drive up the mountain, we stopped at the Big Sky Town Center, and bought some coffee and baked goods. As Professor waited his turn at the bakery, he saw a fox running across the parking lot.

"I just saw a fox!" he exclaimed, as I joined him.

"Where?" I asked, looking all around, hoping to catch a glimpse of the fox.

"He's gone; he ran toward the trees," Professor responded, pointing to the nearby wooded area.

"I wish I had seen him." I was disappointed. I had seen foxes running across the road but never up close.

We got back in the car and continued driving the long, narrow, winding road going up the mountain. Professor had been to the Beehive Basin trail once before, so he was confident that he remembered the directions. We reached a fork in the road and there were no signs for the trail, so Professor guessed and turned right. After passing several large homes, we came to a sharp hairpin turn. The cliff edge was right in front of us with no guard rail – nothing to prevent the car from going over the edge and smashing into the valley below. Professor jammed on the brakes while I grabbed the handle on the car door trying not to scream in terror. I did not want to upset Professor, who was trying to control the car. Professor drove the car slowly around the insanely sharp turn until we found a place to turn around. This was an ominous start to our hike on Beehive Basin trail.

Eventually we found our way and Professor pulled our car into the small parking lot for Beehive Basin trail at 9:15 a.m. The parking lot was almost full and he squeezed our car into one of the few remaining parking spots. This trail has become quite popular since its 2014 designation as one of the 10 best hikes in America.

The trailhead starts at an elevation of about 8,000 feet and climbs up to more than 9,500 feet. Due to the high starting elevation, the hike is moderately difficult meaning most hikers will be short-of-breath as they climb the trail. As the trail climbs, it enters the Spanish Peaks Unit of the Lee Metcalf Wilderness which reminds us of the Teton Range in Wyoming with its characteristic jagged peaks. The views are spectacular and the trail terminates in a remarkable glacial valley with a small, alpine lake.

Professor and I hiked at a moderate pace, passing many large groups of tourists. We stopped at a rocky outcrop where a kind person took our photo with Lone Mountain peak in the background. We are smiling in the photo since our hike was going well at that point.

As we neared the lake at the top, we had to climb a very steep, rocky section of the trail. Even though we had been hiking in Montana all summer at high elevations, we were huffing and puffing in this last section. We had good company. I passed one man who was breathing very hard, his face turning bright red while sweat poured off his head onto the ground. He was leaning on a tree and did not look well.

"I hope that guy doesn't have a heart attack," I said to Professor.

He nodded, trudging ahead. He always walks ahead of me on the trail, lost in his own thoughts.

The views of the lake at the end of the trail were amazing with snow-covered rocks connecting the sparkling lake with the clear blue sky. We found a spot on one of the slopes above the lake away from the crowd while being careful not to step on the multitude of wildflowers in bloom and ate our lunch in silence. When a black cloud stopped over our heads, we decided it was a sign to head back down the trail. The top of a mountain is not a good place to be in a thunderstorm given the high risk of lightning strikes. It was another ominous sign.

Surprisingly, a lot of people were still hiking up to the lake. Halfway down the trail, we sat on a boulder to rest and have a snack. A family with three adults and five small children stopped next to us. They were arguing about whether they should continue hiking up the trail because they had no water. Even though the official temperature was 80 degrees Fahrenheit, the high elevation made the temperature feel much hotter increasing the risk of heat stroke.

I was concerned about this family since they were not carrying any food or water. "Give them one of our extra bottles of water," I said, prodding Professor with my elbow. He scowled, looking uncertain while continuing to listen to the conversation. Finally, he reached in his pack and handed a 16-ounce bottle of water to the man who appeared to be leading the group.

"Great, thanks," the man said abruptly while turning away to talk to the women and children behind him.

Professor nodded as I looked on, hoping they would make the right decision and return to the parking lot. The 16-ounce bottle of water was barely enough water for one person to hike safely back to the parking lot; this was a group of eight people. Unfortunately, they decided the water was enough to sustain them. We watched as the family continued walking slowly up the trail to the lake with the one bottle of water to share among eight people.

Professor and I hiked another mile down the trail and took a break. The temperature was getting hotter so we peeled off our top layer of clothing and sat on a rock underneath limited shade to rest. Even though we were in good physical condition by this point in the summer, we were feeling tired from the strenuous hike through the steep, rocky section of the trail.

"Is it okay if I walk with you?" A small voice piped up next to us. We turned to see a petite, elderly lady perched on a small boulder next to us.

The lady introduced herself as Edna. She wasn't feeling well and she didn't have any food or water. She had already eaten her one snack, a granola bar, and finished her one small bottle of water. We gave her a bottle of our water with electrolytes and some energy chews until she felt better.

As Professor chatted with Edna, I looked at her more closely. She was dressed in the perfect outfit for a Sunday afternoon outing at the golf club – a white visor, dangling earrings, bright pink tank top and white capri pants. The cute sandals on her feet were perfect for sitting under an umbrella with a cool drink but not ideal for hiking on a steep, rocky trail. We started walking down the trail, thinking it was best to get Edna back to the parking lot and her car where she could turn on the air conditioning. She walked very slowly since she was tired and her sandals kept slipping on the rocky trail. Edna talked nonstop and we learned more about the group she was hiking with – her husband, daughter, daughter-in-law and five grandchildren.

"They left you here by yourself?" I asked, incredulous that someone would just leave an elderly lady with very little food and water, to wait several hours by herself while they finished their hike.

"Yes, they wanted to hike to the lake," Edna replied, matter-of-factly.

As Edna filled us in on the details, we realized the people she was describing were the same eight people whom we had previously given a bottle of water. The family was visiting Big Sky on vacation, renting one of the many luxury homes built into the side of a mountain. They read about Beehive

Basin in a magazine and decided to hike to the lake.

"Have you done any hiking before this?" I inquired, wondering what people think when they undertake a strenuous hike with little preparation.

"Yes, we did some hiking in Yellowstone two days ago," Edna replied, earnestly.

Professor and I nodded our heads, looking at each other over Edna's head. We were both thinking the same thing. Edna's family might have turned around if we had not offered them a bottle of water. However, we had assumed, incorrectly, they would realize that one bottle of water was not enough for eight people hiking on a hot July day.

Edna's cell phone rang and I jumped at the noise, surprised that there was a signal on this remote trail.

"Hi Honey," Edna said, sweetly. "Oh, you're near the top. Okay, I will wait for you at the bottom." She put the high-end smartphone back in her pocket. "They're almost at the lake. They will meet me by the car." She turned to continue walking down the trail.

Professor and I followed her silently, still shocked that her family would just leave her alone on the trail. It would probably be at least two more hours before the family returned to the parking lot.

We continued walking slowly down the trail, listening to Edna talk about her vacation, family and life back in Texas. When we arrived at the parking lot around 1:30 p.m., it was very hot. We walked Edna to her car, expecting to help her get in and blast the air conditioner so that she could cool down.

"I don't have the keys to the car," Edna said, brusquely. "My husband has them."

Professor and I looked at each other, too stunned to speak. We should not have been surprised at this point, but I still wondered what Edna's husband was planning to do with the car keys while he was hiking on the trail. We offered to drive Edna to her rental home or to let her sit in our car to cool down. We were determined to wait with her until her family returned since she had finished all of her water and didn't have any food.

Edna shook her head adamantly. "I'll just sit here and wait for them." She sat down on a small rock near their car, in the hot sun, and stuck her chin out stubbornly. "I have my phone," she added.

The phone promptly chirped with a message from her husband, "We are at the top."

Professor can be very persuasive and he did his best to convince Edna that she should sit in our car and cool down. She wouldn't listen – stubbornly shaking her head and insisting that we leave her alone. We gave Edna more water and snacks and then returned to our car.

We went back to the bakery where I ate the largest brownie that I could find in the display case and washed it down with iced coffee. I worried anxiously about Edna and felt like we should have done more for her.

"She wanted us to leave; there was nothing else that we could do," Professor said, trying to reassure me. "There's no reason to feel guilty."

"I know, I feel like we should have done more to help her," I replied, glumly.

We returned to Bozeman, driving through the mountains in the pouring rain as the thunder clouds that had been following us finally let loose. Trouble greeted us at the door, yowling persistently since it was past her dinner time. After giving her some food, which she devoured, she hopped up on my lap to join me in a nap.

For several days after the incident, I kept checking the local news to see if there were any emergency rescues at Beehive Basin. I didn't see any news stories so I assumed that Edna was okay.

I hoped that the rest of our summer adventures would be less stressful, but that was not to be the case.

20 BISON IN OUR TENT

Early on a Tuesday morning, Professor came bursting through the front door loaded down with hiking gear and a fresh cup of espresso from our favorite coffee shop. He had a big smile on his face and was humming an unnamed tune. He had been hiking with a group of friends and it was obvious they had enjoyed themselves.

"How was your hike?" I was sitting at the kitchen table, doing some work. Trouble was stretched out on her favorite rug, basking in the sun streaming through the sliding glass door that opens to the patio.

"It was great! Everyone showed up and we hiked five miles. I met some interesting new people. After hiking, we went to the coffee shop so I brought you some coffee."

I was already taking the cup out of his hands. The air was chilly this morning and the steaming coffee was just what I needed to get warm.

Professor talked excitedly about his morning hike while I sipped my coffee. He enjoys meeting new people and spoke kindly about each of his new friends. I was only half-listening, thinking about the task that I had been doing when he came in the door.

"We should go camping in Yellowstone!" he exclaimed.

"What?" I heard the word "camping" and snapped out of my reverie.

"My friend Dan just came back from a camping trip in Yellowstone. They had a great time and saw all kinds of wildlife. We should go camping; it would be fun!"

"I don't really like camping. Can't we just stay in one of the Yellowstone lodges?"

"The lodges are booked this time of year. We should have made reservations back in March if we wanted to stay at a lodge. Besides, I want to sit around a campfire, roast marshmallows and look at the stars. I want to go camping."

I rolled my eyes. Professor can be hard-headed – stubborn as a mule, or a bison standing in the road blocking traffic.

"Camping in a tent can be a lot of work and it also requires the right gear. We don't even own a tent."

"Dan said we could borrow some of his gear. Also, we can get some used gear from the secondhand sports shops. Let's do it!" Professor's enthusiasm was contagious.

I started thinking about sitting around a campfire, roasting marshmallows and eating s'mores. It was a nice thought until I remembered that the mosquitoes are fierce in Yellowstone in the summer and I am a mosquito magnet.

Professor was determined to go camping, so we made a reservation at the Madison Campground in Yellowstone and borrowed some gear from friends. We found a used tent in a secondhand store and packed some of our bins with basic supplies. Our neighbor agreed to take care of Trouble. Our neighbor has two cats and treats them like her children so I was confident that she would take good care of our cat.

We drove from Bozeman to Yellowstone National Park early on a Friday morning and found our campsite in the Madison Campground next to the Madison River. It was a peaceful spot and we ate lunch at the picnic table in our campsite, excited to be back in Yellowstone. This was our third trip, but the park is so immense there were many areas that we had yet to explore. We hoped that camping would make our stay more efficient. We would get an early start in the morning and beat the traffic coming into the park in the morning from West Yellowstone.

We cooked a simple dinner over an open campfire. I built the fire using skills that I learned during my years as a Girl Scout and gave Professor a lesson on the art of roasting marshmallows. A roasted marshmallow should be brown and crispy on the outside, hot and gooey on the inside. If the marshmallow gets too hot, it becomes a flaming mass resulting in a lump of black charcoal. The process starts with a clean stick which is long enough to reach from your camp chair to the fire. After putting the marshmallow on the stick, ease the stick toward the flames. By keeping the marshmallow near the edge of the flames, it will be perfect for making s'mores with the marshmallow melting the chocolate and sticking to the graham cracker.

We had a relaxing evening sitting around our campfire and reminiscing about past trips to Yellowstone. We hoped to explore some new places and see lots of wildlife.

"This is very relaxing. Why don't you like camping?" Professor stared into the fire as he talked.

"I think I did too much camping as a kid; I got tired of it. Also, I don't usually sleep very well in a tent. The ground is hard and campgrounds can be noisy. Have I told you about my family camping experiences?"

"Your family went camping? It's hard to believe. I am guessing that your sisters didn't like it."

"Well, let me tell you about our camping trips." I continued with my story.

When I was in elementary school, Mom and Dad bought a 20-foot camper. Built in the 1970's, it was decorated with colors that were trendy at the time – lime green, rust and gold. The exterior was white with lime green stripes. The linoleum floor was the same green. The fabric on the couch and table seat cushions was rust. The table and countertops were gold laminate while the refrigerator and trim were the color of wood paneling.

As an adult, I appreciate that we did so much traveling. New York has some awesome outdoor places including the Adirondacks, Watkins Glen, Lake Champlain and of course Niagara Falls. The camper allowed us to go to many of these places. Remembering these experiences, I believe this first taste of the outdoors planted a seed in me which has fully blossomed in midlife

As a kid, I did not like camping in the trailer. The one-room, one-bathroom trailer was too small for a family of five tall people. On a sunny day, we would be outside for most of day, but on a rainy day we would be stuck inside, jammed around the table playing games.

The sleeping arrangements were complicated. My sisters would sleep together on the top bunk and getting into the bed meant climbing a small ladder. Kathy would be squashed in the back against the wall while Shirley was next to her, trying not to fall off the edge with a five-foot drop to the floor. Once they were in bed, you could hear them arguing over space.

"Move over, you're squishing me!"; "Stop kicking me!"; "I don't have room to move!"; "Mom, tell her to stop!" The kicking, pushing and yelling continued until Mom intervened. Dad couldn't move quickly in the trailer; he was too tall. When he got near the bunk beds, he often bumped his head.

My parents slept on the bottom of the bunk beds, underneath my sisters' bed. Mom never slept well so she was usually cranky in the morning. Dad always slept well and his snoring often kept the rest of us awake. I had the best sleeping spot on the other side of the room. The dining table came off its posts and the seat pulled out into a bed.

We spent many summers at a campground on the Great Sacandaga Lake. The campground had a large beach and lots of activities including miniature golf. Dad taught us how to play miniature golf. Since he is left-handed, that's how I learned to play. To this day, I can swing the club from both sides.

After getting sweaty playing golf, we walked down a hill to the beach. Grandma and Grandpa stayed in a cabin near the beach so they joined us. Grandma would put on her best floral swimsuit with a scarf to protect her hair, made into a helmet with lots of hairspray. Grandpa would wear his swim shorts, letting his Santa Claus belly hang out. He enjoyed swimming and spent most of his beach time in the water.

Dad would rent a canoe and we would paddle to an island and sit quietly, soaking up the sun and cool breeze blowing across the lake. I enjoyed the solitude, away from the hub bub of the campground. At those times, I felt like I was in tune with the nature around us.

In the evenings, we would sit around a campfire roasting marshmallows and socializing with friends who were camping nearby. Occasionally, a curious skunk or raccoon would wander into the campsite and Mom would order Dad to chase the animal away.

"These were some of my first outdoor experiences," I said, finishing my story and gazing into the flames of the campfire.

"It sounds like you had fun on your family camping trips." Leave it to Professor to put a positive spin on my memories.

"We had some fun, but it was not enough to make me want to take up camping again."

We went to bed early, putting all of our food and toiletries in the car. Yellowstone has a healthy population of black bears. Although we enjoy seeing them from a distance, we did not want them visiting our campsite. We closed the tent flap and crawled into our sleeping bags. We had only brought basic supplies, so the sleeping bag which seemed warm and cozy when I handled it in the store now seemed to be thin and cold. I could feel every stone on the ground beneath the tent. I felt like the main character in Hans Christian Andersen's *The Princess and the Pea*.

Eventually, I adjusted to my rocky bedding and slept until the sounds and smells of the campground stirring woke me up. I smelled bacon frying in a pan and my stomach started rumbling with the anticipation of breakfast. Professor made a tasty breakfast over the campfire though he burned the pancakes since he underestimated how hot a cast iron pan gets when placed over an open flame.

Fueled with Professor's campfire cooking, we drove to our chosen trailhead and within a short time we were hiking up a hill and looking out over the park. It was a chilly summer morning with a clear blue sky – great hiking weather. We gazed at the summer flowers – a carpet of bright blossoms covering the hillsides.

As we hiked up the hill, we got caught up in our conversation and ignored one of the first rules of the trail – pay attention to your surroundings. We rounded a sharp curve in the trail and stopped quickly. I bumped into Professor and opened my mouth to issue a reproach. I remained silent because there was a huge moose standing right in front of us on the trail. We had come dangerously close to walking into the young male moose.

Professor reacted quickly. "Good morning, nice moose. We won't hurt you – just keep eating your breakfast." He backed away slowly up the hill next to the trail. I followed his example, backing away slowly, feeling very nervous and trying not to trip over anything. The moose continued eating, never raising his head. His eyes moved in our direction and I saw his ears twitch. He was well aware of our presence, but did not appear to be disturbed. Seeing a moose in Yellowstone up close is unusual. However, they are still wild animals, and will take action if they feel threatened.

After climbing up the hill, we walked across the top and then back down onto the trail – far away from the moose. We hiked all day, returning to our tent happy and exhausted. After a simple meal of canned beans and crackers we fell into bed as the campground got dark and quiet. Noisy people pulled into the campground late in the evening, but I was so tired that I was able to ignore them.

I woke up at dawn and decided to walk to the nearby restroom. I crawled out of my warm sleeping bag and put on a hat and jacket to ward off the chill of the early morning. I opened the tent flap and stumbled across the threshold, forgetting to pick up my feet in my half-awake stupor. The cold air hit me in the face. Even in the summer, Yellowstone can have temperatures below freezing at night.

Afterwards, I made my way back to our tent, looking at the ground in the dim light and choosing my steps carefully to avoid tripping and falling. I reached the picnic table in our campsite and looked up, trying to find my way to the tent. I stopped, frozen, unable to move because of shock. Our tent was surrounded by bison.

The bison were everywhere – behind the tent, next to the tent, in the campsites next to us and in the field on the edge of the campground. Out of the corner of my eye, I saw our neighbor in the campsite next to us. He was sitting on top of his picnic table, holding a mug of hot coffee and smiling.

I was panicking. Several bison were standing right next to our tent and one large male was near the back wall of the tent. Professor was lying in his sleeping bag right next to that wall – right next to the bison's hooves. If anything scared the herd, Professor could be trampled through the thin canvas fabric of the tent.

My anxiety-fueled imagination went crazy. I envisioned the bison herd being spooked by some loud noise within the campsite, causing them to run. The startled bison next to our tent raised his head quickly in his rush to evacuate the campsite, catching part of our tent on his horns. As the 2000-pound animal started running, he dragged the tent along with him, with Professor waving his arms wildly and shouting "Help! Help!"

I shook my head, returning to reality. The bison were grazing peacefully, eating the grass near their feet and then taking a few steps forward. They appeared to be following their normal path and were relatively undisturbed by our presence. Still, I was afraid to move; I didn't want to scare them.

Professor's head poked out of the front of the tent. He wasn't dressed so he held the canvas tightly around him, clutching it at the base of his throat. He looked at me with a wide-eyed expression of fascination and fear – the same expression that people have when riding a roller coaster. He poked one finger out of the tent, pointing to the bison behind him. I nodded my head in understanding, afraid to speak. I thought about how this was a great photo opportunity. Surely not too many people have a photo of their husband in a tent surrounded by bison. However, the camera was in the car and I was frozen in fear.

Professor told me later that he woke up when I went to the restroom and then snuggled back into his sleeping bag, intent on going back to sleep. As he lay there dozing, he heard a huffing sound. Half asleep and not one to panic, he continued to lie there trying to decipher the source of the noise. He heard more huffing, then the sounds of hooves stepping on rocks, and the sounds of chewing. By this point, he was fully awake. He moved gingerly across the floor of the tent to the flap and peered out. That was when our eyes met across the campsite.

We sat patiently as the bison finished grazing and moved away from the campground toward the river. We waited until they were out of sight before talking excitedly about our experience. In hindsight, it was one of those unforgettable moments where we truly felt a part of nature.

The rest of the weekend in Yellowstone was uneventful. We returned to our condo to find Trouble sleeping peacefully on the couch. The condo was full of evidence of her weekend escapades. She looked up briefly and greeted me with a soft "meow" and then went back to sleep. She was content so I knew the neighbor had taken good care of her while we were camping in Yellowstone.

21 LEAVING THE WEST

Summer is a short season in Montana. By early August, the air has a chill in the morning and the nights can be cold. The flowers wilt, the leaves on the trees change from green to yellow, red and brown and the mountain ranges look brown. The end of summer also means that we have to drive back to Florida so we can return to our full-time jobs.

Our departure day arrived much too soon and Professor and I were overwhelmed with sadness at leaving our second home. Our summer had been filled with adventure and we felt dejected that our vacation was coming to an end. Trouble weaved in-between my legs and then licked my feet; she didn't want to leave her Montana home either.

The car was packed and Professor and I walked through the condo, going through my checklist for closing up the condo. The water was turned off, the refrigerator was empty except for a few ice cubes, and all of our bins were packed in the back of our SUV. I found Trouble hiding in the second-floor closet and gently put her inside her carrier. She didn't struggle or cry; she knew it was time to go.

I waved to the neighbors as Professor pulled the car out of the parking lot. Professor is usually upbeat and smiling, but as we drove away from the condo, he was silent and morose. Hiking is one of his favorite activities and he wished he could stay longer, do more hiking and meet more new people. Trouble sat silently in the corner of her pet carrier, sharing our thoughtful state.

As we headed out of the city, I saw the sign for I-90 East. "Good-bye, Bozeman. See you next summer." My voice cracked as I felt the heartache, close to a physical pain, at leaving a place that has become an integral part of who we are. There is something special about this place; it has grabbed hold of us and become ingrained into our hearts. We cannot let go, we cannot forget and we leave knowing that we will return soon. We have to come back;

this place is now a part of us.

Professor and I sat silently in the car, driving 70 miles-per-hour on I-90 East through Montana toward Wyoming. Trouble was snoozing in her carrier in the back seat.

"I've got to be where my spirit can run free. Got to find my corner, of the sky." The lyrics from *Corner of the Sky*, a song in the Broadway musical Pippin, were cycling through my mind as we drove through the mountains of Montana. The lyrics are profound, saying what I feel about Montana. It's a place where my spirit is free to roam; a place where the sky is endless, bound only by the peaks of the Rocky Mountains.

After a brief lunch break in Billings, Montana, we were back on the highway. The landscape was changing – more brown than green. As the car crossed the state line into Wyoming, Professor's voice startled me from my silent reflection. "Goodbye Montana; we'll see you next year. Next summer we'll do even more hiking." Professor tried to sound upbeat and optimistic, but I knew he felt dispirited.

I sat sullenly staring out the window at my last glance of Montana until next summer. The sky was clear in Wyoming and the sun shone across my lap, forcing me to remove the pullover that I put on to ward off the early morning chill. The wind whipped across the flat plains creating small dust devils. As I looked across to the Bighorn Mountains in Wyoming, I saw a small, puffy cloud perched at the top. There was no doubt that thunder clouds would be close behind. We always worry about summer thunderstorms and the severe weather that can come with them – flash floods, large hail and tornadoes.

The trip went smoothly and we pulled into the parking lot for the hotel in Buffalo, Wyoming. We stayed in our usual room overlooking the horses in the pasture, but it felt different. In the spring, we were excited, anticipating the possibilities of the summer in Bozeman. Now we just felt like weary travelers, already anxious to get home even though we had only been traveling for one day.

Trouble and I sat by the window, watching the horses grazing in the field behind the hotel. Their tails were swishing in the sunlight, swatting at persistent flies that seemed to be hatching in the nearby stream. Trouble purred contently as I scratched the sweet spot between her shoulders. She had been an excellent traveler and I praised her while hoping that her exemplary behavior would continue.

After dinner, Professor and I strolled along the fence surrounding the field where the horses were grazing.

"See you next year, horses," Professor said, waving to the horses.

I laughed, but then stopped as one of the horses looked at us, perking up his ears. After a moment, the horse went back to grazing in the tall grass and Professor and I walked back to our room. We planned to get an early start the next morning, hoping to beat the summer heat in South Dakota.

We had an uneventful stay in Rapid City, South Dakota and continued driving east on I-90. The Badlands landscape which looked interesting and inviting in the spring now looked like a desert. The sun blazed across the bleached sand and stone radiating heat and Professor turned the air conditioning up to the highest setting.

"Good-bye Badlands; see you next year," Professor said, waving his hand at the exit sign for the park.

We ate our lunch at the rest stop in Chamberlain, South Dakota, enjoying the view and taking time to say "Good-bye" to the Dignity of Earth and Sky statue. We always feel like we are entering the West when we see the statue on our trip to Montana. On our return trip to Florida, we feel like the opposite is true.

As we drove across the state line into Iowa, we were aware of the dramatic change in the landscape. There were no more mountains on the horizon; only endless, flat fields dotted by clumps of trees and the occasional farm building. There were more cars on the road and more people at the rest stops.

Once Trouble was settled in the hotel room in Sioux City, Iowa, Professor and I took our usual walk along the Missouri River. The next day we went into town to complete our errands. "Good-bye, Thomas Jefferson," Professor said to the memorial statue next to the sports store at the mall.

We were back on the road the next day, driving to Iowa City. We left early to try to beat the thunderstorms, but the thunderstorms won the race. The sky filled up with angry black clouds in the early afternoon. I switched to a local radio station and heard the warning for severe thunderstorms in the area including the chance of large hail. Some parts of the state had seen baseball-size hail.

"Did the meteorologist on the radio say there was hail the size of baseballs?" I said, incredulously.

Professor nodded his head, his brows squeezed together in concentration as he drove the car in the pounding rain. On the horizon, we saw jagged bolts of lightning reaching between the sky and the ground. It was a spectacular show of nature and we were driving right into the center.

We arrived at our hotel in Iowa City late in the afternoon and followed our usual hotel routine. I stood by the window watching the storm on the horizon, noticing that the blackest clouds were north of us and seemed to be heading away from our hotel. "Maybe the worst of the storm will pass us by," I suggested, optimistically.

Professor was watching the news on television, showing pictures of property damage from the baseball-size hail. "I hope you're right because this looks like a nasty storm." Professor scowled at the pictures of the damage to cars caused by the large hail.

Trouble hopped up on the windowsill next to me and gazed out at the black clouds which now appeared to be reaching down to the ground, like a tornado funnel. The cat jumped off the windowsill, ran to the couch and buried herself under the pillows.

"That's not good!" I was getting more concerned about the weather.

"What's the matter?" Professor asked, his eyes still focused on the television.

"Trouble is hiding under the pillows. That's what she does at home when there is a tornado warning."

Professor looked out the window and then back at the television. "We'll have to wait and see what happens with the weather."

I knew he was worried about our car since there was no shelter for cars at the hotel. We felt helpless – waiting and watching to see what the storm would do. We went to bed in the middle of the storm, exhausted from traveling, but sleeping fitfully as we worried about the violent weather.

Trouble was awake at 5 a.m., rubbing her head against my cheek. She had not eaten much of her dinner since she was hiding from the storm. I could hear her stomach growling in my ear. I gave Trouble her breakfast and looked out the window, watching the colorful sunrise and hoping that our car was not damaged. I could not imagine what we would do if our car needed major repairs.

Professor checked on our car before eating breakfast; it was not damaged. Later in the day, we saw many cars and trucks with baseball-size dents and cracked windshields. If that had happened to our car, we would have been stuck in Iowa until our car could be repaired, trying to get new hotel reservations at all of the remaining stops along our route. This would be challenging because the pet rooms are usually booked in the summer.

We stopped at one of Professor's favorite highway rest areas in Iowa. As he turned the car onto the road leading to the parking area, Professor began his annual lecture on Interstate Highway System rest areas.

"The history of highway rest areas parallels the car culture in America. In the 20th century, mass production and lower costs meant that more families could afford to own a car. With more cars came the need for more roads. Congress passed the first road bill in 1921, The Federal Highway Aid Act, which aimed to stitch together the country with a series of primary roads."

Professor stopped talking as he pulled the car into a parking space. We got out of the car and followed the Litter Box Routine.

Professor continued with his lecture as we stretched our stiff limbs. "As the road system expanded, safe places to stop and rest became increasingly important. After President Eisenhower signed the 1956 Federal Highway Aid Act, the National System of Interstate and Military Highways was created. This plan included high-speed, limited access roads crisscrossing America. In 1958, a policy was published to standardize the design of 'safe rest areas.' Safe rest areas had to supply drivers with parking facilities, access to water and restrooms, and safe entrance and exit. Architects began developing unique and creative ideas for rest area designs that incorporated local physical features, landmarks, and culture."

As Professor droned on about the history of rest areas, I thought about how important they are for our trip across the U.S. They provide clean bathrooms, picnic benches, and sometimes include walking trails and pet exercise areas. The rest areas also allow Trouble to take a break from the vibrations of the moving car. While we ate lunch in the picnic area, Trouble put her face in the cool, fresh air from the open car window. This rest area in Iowa is also quiet since it sits away from the highway and has separate parking for large trucks.

Many states continue to design rest areas as interesting stopping points. Rest areas in South Dakota have teepees covering the picnic tables as a reminder of the Native American tribes from the American Great Plains. The rest area in Chamberlain, South Dakota has the information center, the Native American statue and overlooks the Missouri River on a tall bluff.

I appreciate the architecture, scenery, trails and picnic areas at rest stops. However, the most important thing for me on this trip is that they allow us to stop and take care of our cat. Unfortunately, some states are doing away with rest areas to save money. We noticed that Indiana had only a few rest areas while many were closed in Illinois.

On a previous trip, we desperately needed a rest area and couldn't find one. Trouble was yowling because her litter box was dirty and Professor needed a break because he was exhausted from driving. We ended up stopping at a local hotel and paying for one night's stay just so we could take a nap for a few hours in the afternoon. I was too embarrassed to go with Professor to the front desk of the hotel. I could only imagine what the hotel employees thought when he said we needed a room for a few hours so we could "take a nap."

As we said "Good-bye" to Iowa and the excellent rest stops, we talked about our upcoming stay with Mom and Dad. We looked forward to relaxing and getting caught up on our sleep. We would also be able to hear more about the cat drama in their neighborhood.

Trouble pressed her face against the mesh on the cat carrier and purred, appearing to share my thoughts. I was certain that she sensed my pleasant feelings and knew she would be happily settled in Mom and Dad's bedroom by the end of the day.

22 CAT DRAMA

We arrived on schedule at Mom and Dad's house in Ohio. Professor was exhausted so he took a nap in the bedroom while Trouble snuggled against his leg. I sat on the porch with Mom, getting an update on the neighborhood's cat drama.

Mom and Dad live right next to a regional park which has a large population of stray and feral cats. No one seems to know where all of the cats come from. Many of the cats appear to be former house cats, not used to having to feed themselves. My theory is that some people move away without taking their cats while other people use the park as a place to get rid of cats they no longer want. Mom and Dad's house is the first stop for these cats who are looking for food and loving care.

Mom and Dad feed the cats because they cannot resist the sad, hungry faces on the cats sitting on their doorstep and peering in the glass storm door. Mom has tried to address the situation by trapping the cats and getting them spayed and neutered at a local nonprofit organization and releasing them.

Many of the neighbors have adopted cats so the neighborhood now has a small population of outdoor domestic cats in addition to the stray and feral cats. Some of the cats are friendly and live very well. They go from house to house looking for a meal. One morning, I opened the front door and saw four cat faces pressed against the glass storm door.

"Oh, what is this?" I asked, peering down at the adorable fuzzy faces.

"That's Binky, Grayson, Tiger and Wally Clipper," Dad said, pointing to each of the cats and rattling the names off quickly. "Of course, the neighbors have different names for them. Everyone feeds them."

"That's very interesting," I replied slowly, still processing the information.

"Hello, kitties!" Mom exclaimed, rushing to the door. The four cat faces looked up, blinking their eyes to smile at my mother. These cats know how to get what they want.

"Time for breakfast, kitties!" Mom stepped out the door and placed a paper plate filled with dry cat food and leftover table food, including chicken and scrambled eggs, near the cats.

One of the feral cats is named "Mama Cat." She eats the food in a dish on the doorstep, but she avoids the food in a trap. Mom has not been able to catch this cat and so she has not been spayed. Mama Cat is petite, with long, thick white fur and patches of gray stripes splashed across the white fur. Her favorite mate is Tom – another cat who has also cleverly avoided the trap. Mama Cat and Tom have produced several litters of kittens – tiny balls of white fur with patches of gray stripes.

In one recent litter, Mama Cat had three kittens. The tiny creatures were adorable, but Mama Cat did not seem interested in caring for them. She made a home under the shed on the other side of Mom and Dad's fence. Mama Cat stayed under the shed while the tiny kittens wandered around the yard. The owner of the property, a busy police officer, was oblivious to the activities of the feline family.

Mom and Dad enjoy gardening and spend a great deal of time in their backyard. They watched the kittens exploring the neighbor's yard with growing apprehension. The neighbor had a pool which was uncovered for spring cleaning. On one bright spring afternoon, Mom and Dad were planting their flowers when they heard an unusual noise.

"What's that noise?" Mom asked, scowling. She is sensitive to any kind of noise, particularly high-pitched sounds.

"I don't hear anything," Dad replied, pulling a weed out of the ground. He needs hearing aids after spending years working around planes during his service in the Air Force, but he rarely wears them.

Mom was not deterred. She followed the sound, looked over the fence and was horrified at what she saw.

"Look!" Mom cried, pointing her finger at the neighbor's pool.

"Oh no!" Dad yelled, finally understanding what was happening. One of the kittens had fallen into the pool. The kitten was crying – loud, shrieking cries. Mama Cat sat under the shed, ignoring the plight of her kitten. The other two kittens watched curiously, not sure how to react.

"We have to do something!" Mom shouted, near tears at the sight of the tiny kitten being swallowed up by the water in the pool. They stood helplessly next to the high fence, unable to rescue the kitten.

Dad was already running into the house as fast as his 75-year-old knobby knees would take him. He called the police officer's home phone number, but there was no answer.

By the time Dad returned to the yard, the kitten's cries had stopped. Mom was standing motionless by the fence, tears running down her cheeks. Dad understood the situation immediately, and his eyes welled up. He loves all of the cats – domestic, stray and feral. Watching the kitten drown was traumatic and Dad says he can still hear the kitten's cries in his mind when he thinks about the tragedy.

Mom and Dad were horrified. Even though this was just one more feral kitten, they could not tolerate seeing its life ended so tragically. As they watched the other two kittens crying for their sibling who was floating lifeless in the pool, they decided to take action. Mom called the neighbor when he arrived home and watched as he took the dead kitten out of the pool and put it in the trash bin.

"Do you mind if we take the other two kittens?" Mom asked politely while trying to contain her anger. "The mother is not taking care of them."

"No, take them," the neighbor replied gruffly. He was too busy to worry about kittens in his backyard and was glad when Mom and Dad offered to take care of the problem.

Mom and Dad took the kittens and started caring for them, feeding them milk through an eyedropper until they could drink milk out of a dish. The kittens would sit on the sunporch and cry for their mother. Suddenly, Mama Cat was interested in her kittens, sitting outside the screened porch crying for her kittens. Mom remembered how Mama Cat watched the other kitten drown and would not let the kittens near the mother.

My niece was devoted to the kittens and named them Emmie and Timmie. She spent endless hours playing with them – holding and cuddling them. The kittens appeared to be healthy, but they had been feral cats for six weeks, so they needed some medical care. Mom is a nurse, so when Emmie showed signs of an eye infection, she noticed it immediately. The veterinarian said the infection was too far gone to be treated with antibiotics; the eye had to be removed or the infection would spread beyond the eye. Mom was distraught. Emmie would die without the eye surgery, but Mom could not afford to pay for the surgery.

A kind woman from Mom and Dad's church offered to pay for the surgery. She didn't want the kittens, but she loved cats and was compassionate about Emmie's plight. The vet removed Emmie's eye and stitched the socket closed. Emmie healed quickly from the procedure and didn't seem to mind having one eye. She learned to open her single eye wider to compensate for the loss of the other eye. With her other eye socket stitched closed, she appears to be winking at the world around her. She continued to be a happy, healthy, playful kitten, tumbling across the room with Timmie.

Mom and Dad already had two cats, Molly and Smoky, so they tried to find a home for the kittens. No one wanted to adopt the kittens and Mom did not want to separate the siblings. Eventually, Mom found a nonprofit organization managed by a kind lady who promised to find a good home for them. She assured Mom she would try to keep the kittens together. Mom gave the kittens to the lady, feeling like she had no other choice.

By this time, my niece and nephew, who live a few minutes away, had become very attached to the kittens. My niece was in tears when she went to visit my parents and the kittens were not there. My sister Kathy finally acquiesced so Mom went back to the nonprofit and adopted the kittens. She had to pay an adoption fee to take them home, but Emmie and Timmie became permanent members of our family.

My niece took over the care and feeding of both kittens and my nephew took on the role of primary teaser. The kittens were cuddled, pampered, groomed and carried around the house. They were so trusting, relaxed and happy that they were like rag dolls; anyone could pick them up and hold them and they would stay very relaxed. My niece played with them like baby dolls – dressing them up in doll clothes and posing them for photos. The kittens sat patiently in their dresses and hats while my sister captured the moment in a photo.

Emmie and Timmie were mischievous kittens. When they were left alone, they would get into all kinds of things. One day, my sister came home to find peanuts strewn all about the kitchen. The cats tipped over the can that was on the counter, playing with peanuts, scooting them across the kitchen floor and then eating them. The next day, Emmie and Timmie didn't feel well.

One afternoon, Kathy left a homemade peach pie on the counter to cool while she ran errands. She came home to find the kittens covered in peach pie. The pie was destroyed and had to be thrown in the trash. The kittens needed a bath to remove the sticky peach filling from their long fluffy fur.

Emmie and Timmie continued to be close, sleeping together curled into a fluffy white ball and grooming each other. Emmie always stepped aside if Timmie wanted to eat some of her food. She was more timid, wary because of her single eye. Timmie was more adventurous; a curious cat who liked to explore new places. One afternoon, the family came home and couldn't find Timmie. They looked in all of the usual hiding places, but the cat wasn't there. Emmie sat by the screen door looking out into the backyard, crying for Timmie. My niece was in tears, fearing something terrible had happened to the cat.

As they sat in the kitchen, staring dejectedly at their cups of green tea, they heard the sound of a cat crying. The sound seemed to be far away, so they thought it was the neighbor's Scottish Fold cat who often stops by for a visit. Then they realized the sound was coming from under the deck.

My niece rushed out the door, forgetting shoes and a jacket, calling, "Timmie! Timmie!" and the cat's howling got louder. Crawling in the mud under the deck, she found Timmie squeezed into a dark corner, shivering and covered with mud. Timmie had escaped through a hole in the screen door, explored the dark, muddy area under the deck and then lost her way.

My niece and Timmie went straight to the bathtub. After a shampoo, blow-dry and a snack, Timmie curled up on a blanket for a long nap.

Emmie is calmer than Timmie; she is all sweetness, enjoying long naps in my niece's lap or just sitting next to my niece while she does her homework. On Valentine's Day, they sent me a picture of Emmie, appearing to sit up with her paws holding a creative Valentine's Day card. I could see my niece's arms behind the cat, propping her up for the photo.

Emmie and Timmie are now beloved members of the family, but this story was only the beginning. The number of cats in Mom and Dad's neighborhood continued to multiply, causing a myriad of issues and a continuing cat drama.

23 GOOD-BYE GRANDMA

After a couple of days at Mom and Dad's house, we felt rested and ready to continue on our trip back to Florida. Trouble was very relaxed and hid under the bed while we were packing the car. She wanted to continue staying with Mom and Dad.

As we crossed the Ohio border, going into West Virginia and then on to Virginia, I thought about Grandma. I felt miserable after traveling for a week in the car, but Grandma would have loved this car trip. She enjoyed driving and she loved cats. I imagined Grandma sitting in the backseat of the car, petting Trouble who would purr loudly and contently.

Grandma had compassion for all creatures, possibly because she grew up in the mountains and animals were always part of the extended family. For as long as I can remember, Grandma had a cat. One cat, Spider, was a very fat calico since Grandpa was a chef who was generous with the kitchen scraps. As a kid, I would try to pick Spider up, but she was too heavy.

After Grandpa died, Grandma lived by herself, feeling very lonely since she was used to being surrounded by family members. She routinely called our house at 6 p.m., interrupting our dinner because she didn't like eating by herself. To help combat Grandma's loneliness, Mom and Dad gave her a calico cat from the Humane Society. Buttons was a colorful cat with a sweet face and a feisty temperament, often swatting at my hand when I reached down to pet her. This cat was different with Grandma, following her around the house and waiting for her to sit down. As soon as Grandma settled into her arm chair to work on a crochet project, Buttons was by her feet. She would leap into Grandma's lap and curl up with her tail covering her nose. Soon the pair would be napping peacefully together.

Grandma understood the bond between humans and their pets. Buttons worked magic on Grandma, helping her to feel less lonely. Grandma adored Buttons and routinely updated me on the cat's activities. "Buttons greeted me at the door today," she wrote in one letter. Grandma and her cat had long conversations while Grandma drank her coffee in the morning or sipped her sherry in the evening. Buttons was always there when Grandma was alone, missing Grandpa and reminiscing about the days when she had a house full of rambunctious boys.

Science supports what pet owners already know; animals and humans benefit physically and emotionally from the relationship. When a person pets a cat, their blood pressure goes down and the cat's blood pressure also goes down. I believe the science only tells one side of the story. These creatures give us unconditional love and companionship which benefit us in ways that we do not fully understand; just ask anyone with a beloved pet.

When Grandma turned 80, she was no longer able to live independently. By the time she moved to an assisted living home, she had been declining for several years. At first, no one noticed. She forgot to do certain things or was confused about an everyday habit. We overlooked those things and laughed about them. "She's elderly, that's all," I often said. "Everyone has trouble remembering things as they get older."

Eventually, it was impossible to ignore the signs of decline. Grandma lost a lot of weight in a short period of time. After multiple trips to the doctor, there was still no medical explanation.

Mom was determined to find the reason for Grandma's weight loss. "What did you eat for breakfast?" Mom demanded.

"I had a bowl of oatmeal, half a grapefruit and orange juice," Grandma replied, without hesitation.

"And for lunch?" Mom pressed on.

"Tuna salad with salty crackers." Grandma enjoyed eating simple foods, a habit from growing up in a poor family.

Everyone, including the family doctor, was baffled. Mom started filling Grandma's refrigerator with protein shakes. "You need to gain some weight," Mom ordered, reminding Grandma to drink several shakes each day. When Mom went into the kitchen to refill the shake supply, she found the grapefruit rotting in the refrigerator, sour milk and moldy crackers. Grandma was not eating any food.

Mom yelled at the doctor when he diagnosed Grandma with dementia. Even though the evidence was right in front of us, it was unbelievable. Soon it was obvious that Grandma could no longer live independently.

Assisted living was the next best choice. Moving to assisted living was a big adjustment for Grandma. She valued her independence and was very attached to her apartment, her neighbors and her car. She always loved driving; something she didn't learn until age 35. Learning to drive gave her a whole new view of the world – freedom to travel at her own pleasure and convenience.

When Grandma moved into the assisted living community, Buttons had to go to a new home. Parting with her beloved cat was traumatic for Grandma; Buttons was her constant companion. Mom found a home for the cat with a kind family. Grandma met the people and was satisfied that Buttons would have a good home. However, I noticed a marked decline in Grandma's mental health after the cat's departure. She missed her companion. Buttons didn't fare well either, dying a short time later even though she was a young cat. We did not tell Grandma that Buttons died. There was a strong bond between Grandma and Buttons so when the bond was severed, it caused harm to both of them.

After a couple of years in assisted living, Grandma's health declined further. Once she required 24-hour care, she moved to a nursing home near Mom and Dad's house in Ohio.

The last time I saw Grandma, she was in the nursing home. I went to visit her with Dad, who was worn down by the stress of watching his mother fade away slowly. The nursing home was bright, clean and appeared to be well-managed. Even so, as we walked through the front door of the nursing home, I wrinkled my nose. The air was stale with the smell of urine, strong cleaners and other uncomfortable smells. No one likes nursing homes — especially the people who live there.

It was Thanksgiving Day, so all of the residents were in the dining area waiting for their holiday dinners. The nursing home was eerily quiet; there was little conversation and no laughter. Many of the residents were sitting alone — no friends or family members visiting them.

I saw Grandma sitting at a table and tried to smile and be cheerful. Grandma was always ready to give us a big hug. In the past, she would have moved quickly toward me to give me a special Grandma embrace. This time, Grandma didn't move; she just stared straight ahead.

"Hi Grandma," I said, forcing myself to continue smiling while giving her a big hug. As I pulled away, my heart twisted in pain. She looked at me with a blank expression and only a hint of recognition in her eyes. She didn't speak. This was unusual for Grandma, who always loved to talk. She could carry on a phone conversation for an hour all by herself.

As we sat down to the Thanksgiving dinner, a plate full of traditional foods which looked and smelled like cafeteria food, I studied Grandma more carefully. She was almost unrecognizable from the Grandma I had known for 40 years. Grandma always took pride in her appearance. She never left the house before she was ready for a public appearance. Her hair, dyed pale blond, would be fluffed and curled in a style typical of older women. Rose pink lipstick and pink blush brightened her face. Her earrings and necklace always matched, complementing her outfit. Her purse and shoes were dark or light in color, depending on the season. If she was going to work or church, she would wear a suit with a skirt; pants were only for casual days. Her favorite suit was bright fuchsia; a vibrant color that matched Grandma's joy for living. The final touch would be a spritz of her favorite perfume; a scent that still brings tears to my eyes 14 years later.

The Grandma sitting in front of me was wearing a sweatshirt, loose knit pants, and gray sneakers. Her hair was white and messy as if she had just gotten out of bed and she wasn't wearing any makeup or jewelry. She didn't look like my Grandma.

As I sat there feeling helpless and fighting the urge to run out the door, Dad coaxed Grandma into eating some of her food. She didn't seem interested in the food and I couldn't blame her; the food looked unappetizing. Still, she needed to eat and Dad encouraged her until she took a few bites. She sat looking straight ahead while she chewed the over-cooked food – no emotion on her face. Looking into her eyes, I could see that she had given up. Grandma no longer cared if she lived or died.

It won't be much longer, I thought and then felt horrible for having such a morbid thought. Still, I knew instinctively that if she could speak, she would say that she was "ready to be with the Lord" and to "see my husband again."

At the end of our visit, I gave Grandma another big hug. "We'll be back tomorrow, Grandma," I promised. However, we didn't go back. We got busy doing other things for the holiday weekend – shopping on Black Friday, visiting with family, helping my parents around the house. Soon it was time for Professor and I to drive back to Florida and I had only visited Grandma for a couple of hours on Thanksgiving Day.

On the drive back to Florida, I berated myself. *I should have gone back to visit Grandma again during the weekend,* I thought. I kept thinking about the sad look in her eyes and how she must feel – lonesome and unwanted. I still feel guilty every time I think about it.

A few weeks later, Grandma became very ill with pneumonia. With such a dangerous and contagious disease, she was isolated in her room; the only companionship from the gruff, impersonal nursing home staff. Mom and Dad visited Grandma, but they were also elderly and afraid of catching the pneumonia.

"She's all by herself!" Mom was distraught when she called me to update me on Grandma's status. "You know she doesn't like being by herself. This is not good for her overall health."

I felt helpless. There was nothing that I could do but wait and hope. Grandma died a few days later. Pneumonia was the official cause of death, but I was certain Grandma had made up her mind long before that date that it was her last year on earth. She always said, "I never want to be a burden on my family." I know she would have felt like a burden, staying in a nursing home. Even though Medicare paid the bill, she would have felt like she was disrupting Dad's routine when he came to visit her every day.

When Mom called to tell me that Grandma was gone, I cried all night.

Returning my thoughts to the present, I leaned back in my seat in the car and felt a tear slide down my face. Grandma has been gone for close to 14 years, yet some days the pain feels like she just died.

"Are you okay?" Professor was talking while I sat quietly with my memories of Grandma.

"Yes, I'm okay; just weary from driving." I decided to keep my thoughts to myself. He was also tired and we still had two more days of driving until we arrived home in Florida.

I turned around to look in the cat's carrier in the backseat. I couldn't see Trouble, just a pile of sheets. She was buried under the sheets, but when I called, "Trouble? Are you okay, kitty?" she started purring. I knew she was okay, even if she was also tired of traveling.

"We'll be home soon, Trouble," I added, thinking that it would not be soon enough for my cramped legs and sore lower back.

24 FLORIDA HURRICANES

Our trip through the Southeastern states went smoothly. When we crossed the state line into Florida, Professor and I laughed and cheered. "Yay! We're almost home!" The noise woke up Trouble who was napping and she started yowling. She was ready to get home to her cozy napping spots near the warm, sunny windows in our house. The windows are bright with the Florida sunshine in the summer – until the next hurricane arrives.

We arrived home in Jacksonville on a Friday afternoon; the temperature was 96 degrees Fahrenheit with 90 percent humidity, feeling like 105 degrees. For us, the heat was suffocating after the cool, dry air in Montana. We were ecstatic to be home after our long trek. We had successfully traveled with our cat across 13 states for a total of 5,200 miles round trip. This was worth a moment of celebration.

We put Trouble in the house before unpacking the car. I hugged her and praised her heartily, telling her that she was a "good cat" during the trip. She squawked until I put her down and then raced around the house, going to all of her favorite spots as if to say, "I missed you!" Then she sat by her empty food bowl, sighing expectantly. She was hungry after her long trip across the country.

As Professor started unpacking the car, I worked on getting our house in order and then checked the weather forecast on my smartphone. There was a hurricane on the radar and it was heading toward Florida.

Here we go again, I thought, my exuberance at arriving home fading away. After living in Florida for 20 years, we had experienced many tropical storms and hurricanes. Anxiety and fear welled up in my chest and I got a headache as I started thinking about preparing for the storm. I have never gotten used to these storms and they seem to be increasing in number and intensity.

I read more about the current storm. Hurricane Dorian was expected to impact Florida, so I started paying close attention to the National Hurricane

Center's forecast, looking at the arrow with the projected path multiple times throughout the day. We become amateur meteorologists, checking the news, trying to predict the path and intensity of the storm and hoping it will not affect us.

Since it was Labor Day weekend, Professor reminded me of the Labor Day party that we had back in 2004. We had invited friends and colleagues over for a holiday barbecue. On the day of the party, Hurricane Frances was moving into our area, with high winds and heavy rain, so no one showed up at the scheduled time. Then the electricity started going out around town and our phone started ringing. "Do you have power?" people asked. Our electricity was flickering, but it was still on. Once people found out that we had food and electricity, they came to what is now known as our Labor Day Hurricane Party.

That same year, North Florida had a number of consecutive storms, including Bonnie, Charley, Frances, Jeanne and Ivan. I was teaching a class on Wednesday evenings and each week we talked about the storm that had just passed and the storm that was on the radar, heading toward us. We had so many storms in 2004, that the city could not keep up with the debris removal and the streets were lined with huge piles of debris. When Professor and I took our evening walks, we felt like we were walking through a tunnel.

Eventually, the repairs were finished, the debris was cleaned up and life returned to normal including several blissful years with no storms. As each year went by without any severe storms, we became more complacent. The hurricane supplies were pushed to the back of the closet with the batteries and flashlights deteriorating. The wood for covering the windows, sitting in the corner of the garage, became warped and useless. It was easy to forget about the risk of hurricanes after a few years without any storms. The bad memories were pushed deep into our subconscious with a host of other forgotten thoughts.

Life changed dramatically in October 2016 when Hurricane Matthew came up the East coast of Florida. Hurricane Matthew passed by Northeast Florida, 50 miles off the coast. Since it was a large storm, we had rain and strong winds, with gusts up to 80 miles per hour throughout the night. The electricity went off early in the evening, so Professor and I sat in the dark with three flashlights creating a soft glow in the pitch-black darkness. We crouched near the emergency crank radio and took turns winding it, the crank sounding like a large swarm of bees. A local radio station hosted a call-in show, taking phone calls from people all over the area, tracking the path and intensity of the hurricane. This was how we got our news on Hurricane Matthew's impact on our area.

Matthew was the most powerful storm that we had experienced since we moved to Florida. We assumed it was an anomaly and we would be safe for many more years before we had to worry about another hurricane. We were wrong. Less than one year later, in September, 2017, Tropical Storm Irma popped up on the radar. Irma rapidly intensified to a Category 5 hurricane and broke records. This hurricane had the highest sustained intensity for the longest duration. Irma plowed through the Caribbean as a Category 5, causing tremendous destruction of property and loss of life. The pictures on the news were shocking. Many places looked like a bomb had been dropped on them – a total and complete obliteration of structures.

Professor and I followed our storm preparation process, taking storm supplies out of the closet. We needed a few things so I went to the store which was jam-packed with people. I passed a man who had a grocery cart full of potato chips and cases of beer. The stores quickly ran out of bottled water, batteries, flashlights, generators and plywood as people panicked.

Three days before the storm, I went to the gym to get some exercise before being cooped up in the house during the storm. The ten televisions in the gym were showing the news and pictures of the massive hurricane. As I stood and watched the satellite images of the massive hurricane, I was frozen with fear.

As Hurricane Irma came closer, the forecast showed it passing over our house as a Category 2 or 3 hurricane, with winds blowing 96 to 129 miles-per-hour. Professor and I started having intense conversations about going to a storm shelter. In our area, we have several public schools that are shelters, but only one allows pets and it fills up quickly. Going to a shelter with Trouble would mean putting her in the pet carrier with a litter box just like when we drive to Montana. She is used to that routine, but once the car stops and we get into a hotel room, she has her freedom. In a shelter, our cat would have to remain in the carrier.

We have never been to a storm shelter, but from the pictures on television, they appear to be very crowded with people and their belongings. I could imagine the noise and chaos of a large school gymnasium filled with stressed-out families. In a storm shelter, the pets are placed in a separate room. This would be a room filled with dogs, cats, rabbits, etc., stressed out from the hurricane, being separated from their owners and the noise and smells from the other animals. Trouble doesn't get along with other cats and the sound of a dog barking sends her running for cover. She would be petrified; yowling and clawing the black mesh on the side of the carrier.

Professor and I continued to debate our storm plans. As usual, I imagined the worst-case scenario and he was optimistic even in the face of a powerful hurricane.

"What if we have a Category 3 or Category 4 hurricane? With winds over 100 miles-per- hour, we can't stay in our house; it would be too dangerous," I argued.

"We would have to go to a shelter," Professor replied, trying to counteract my overwhelming anxiety.

"What if we can't get into a shelter that takes pets? Those shelters fill up first."

"Then we would have to leave Trouble in the house, while we went to a shelter."

"What?"

"We would leave Trouble in the house."

"Are you crazy? I can't leave the cat by herself in the house!"

"Ginnie, we might not have a choice."

I stared at Professor while imagining what would happen if we left Trouble alone in the house during a powerful hurricane. She would be terrified and probably hide in a closet; one of the safest places in the house. After a powerful storm, there would probably be broken windows. The cat would be scared and would want to get out of the house, going through an open window. The neighborhood would be full of debris and she might get injured or lost.

After discussing all of the options while Hurricane Irma kept moving toward us, we decided to stay in our house. We continued making our preparations – covering our windows with plywood, taking the birdhouses down and putting the sunroom furniture in the garage. The sunroom roof is only rated to withstand sustained wind blowing at 75 miles-per-hour, which means it could blow off with stronger wind gusts. A Category 1 hurricane has winds up to 95 miles-per-hour, so we worried about the sunroom.

By Saturday, September 9th, the National Hurricane Center showed the storm going up the west coast of Florida. This forecast was more favorable for us. However, Trouble's behavior was very strange. She was skittish, jumping at even the slightest sound. She kept looking for hiding places, like she does in a hotel room. She didn't eat very much and seemed very upset. This made me more nervous; I was wondering what it was that she sensed. We finished our storm preparations and prepared to hunker down.

On Sunday, September 10th, the wind increased and the rain pounded the house. There was a nor'easter off the east coast of Florida that was sending lots of rain over Jacksonville. This storm was combining with the outer bands of Hurricane Irma, bringing heavy rains throughout the day and into the night. By sundown, our backyard looked like a lake and the street was flooded. Still, we didn't worry too much because the forecast showed the hurricane tracking west of Jacksonville.

We still had electricity and were stuck in the house, so we watched the endless news cycle as meteorologists analyzed computer models and news cameras showed the destruction from the storm on the Caribbean Islands. It's probably best to avoid watching pictures of devastation from a hurricane when one is bearing down on you, but the damage was unbelievable and it was difficult not to watch the news.

At 11 p.m., we were watching the local news station with meteorologist Mike Buresh. He was talking about Hurricane Irma, which at this point had made landfall in Southwest Florida as a Category 3 hurricane. We could see from the satellite photos that the storm was not following the path projected by the National Hurricane Center. Mike drew a yellow line on the screen showing Irma's projected path; the storm would go right over our house.

We were exhausted from our storm preparations so we went to bed. I woke up at 2:30 a.m.; the wind was howling and the rain was pounding the roof and the windows. The electricity went out and the room was so dark that I couldn't see my hand when I held it up in front of my face. I could hear the hurricane straps flexing and creaking. These straps are designed so the roof moves in the wind and stays attached to the house. So, the groaning sounds of the straps should be reassuring, but the noise just added to my anxiety. Our cellphones were making all kinds of noises: hurricane warnings, tornado warnings, and flood warnings. I picked up my smartphone and stared at the radar. Mike Buresh was right – the storm was coming right at us. It was surreal to watch the massive storm on the phone screen as it moved toward us.

Trouble was running around the house, climbing on top of the kitchen cabinets and searching for places to hide. I heard her metal name tag clanking on her food bowl. When she is very anxious, she licks the bowl clean of every last morsel of food. The wind and rain continued for several more hours and then calmed down. I fell asleep around 5 a.m. and woke up late in the morning. It was eerily quiet; only the sounds of a few chainsaws. A small ray of sunlight was peeking through the corner of the window that was not covered with plywood.

As Professor continued to sleep, I forced myself to get out of bed and check for storm damage. The wind gusts for Irma were estimated at 80 miles per hour and higher so I braced myself, expecting to find a pile of twisted metal instead of the sunroom.

I fed Trouble dry cat food since we still did not have electricity and I didn't want to open the refrigerator. When I walked out to the sunroom, I felt tremendous relief when I found it intact. I could see debris all over the backyard, but no trees were down. I started to relax until I looked out at the front yard; there was water everywhere. The street looked like a river and the water covered half of our yard and driveway. This was unbelievable; we have had flooding in our street in the past, but nothing like this.

We ate a cold breakfast, being careful to keep the refrigerator closed to keep the food cold. In the 21st century, we rely extensively on electricity and connection to the internet so when we don't have them, we feel lost and disconnected. The most frustrating part of not having electricity is not knowing when power will be restored.

Trouble flopped on the couch and then slept all day. The electricity came back on in the afternoon, but we were stranded since the water in our street was too deep for our car. We started cleaning up the debris in the yard and getting the house back in order. After removing the plywood on the windows, Professor discovered that one window was broken. Miraculously, this was the only damage to our house.

We turned on the television to get the news from other parts of the city and state; the pictures were shocking. The news camera showed a sign for Memorial Park, a large city park on the St. Johns River. It's a popular spot for fishing, picnics, walking dogs and sunbathing. That day, the Memorial Park sign looked like it was in the middle of the ocean. All we could see was water and large waves were washing over the sign. The flooding was unprecedented.

Next the news cameras went to Vilano Beach in St. Augustine. This beach is one of Professor's favorite fishing spots. We like to go there on a cool, sunny day and relax before having dinner at a restaurant in the historical City of St. Augustine. Professor has caught all kinds of fish including sand sharks and a baby hammerhead shark. He throws all of the fish back in the ocean, but he enjoys the challenges of the sport. The news cameras showed houses on Vilano Beach that had been demolished by the wind and water. One house was lying on its side with the front door facing the sky.

Around the state there was severe flooding and damage; over a million people did not have power. Scenes from the Florida Keys showed what appeared to be a war zone. The area was devastated, with a few homes standing in the middle of the piles of wood and debris. It was shocking to see the photos of places that we know so well, with such extensive damage. Many people could not get back to their homes as bridges remained closed to assess damage from the storm.

Professor and I felt fortunate; our property damage was minor compared to what many people suffered. Many individuals and businesses were still recovering from Hurricane Matthew when Hurricane Irma hit. The cleanup process would take more than a year.

Returning our focus to 2019, we unpacked from our recent trip to Montana as Hurricane Dorian passed by bringing only a little wind and rain. Grateful to have avoided another hurricane, we settled back into our daily routine. In the fall, we can truly enjoy the Florida weather, getting outside to walk in the parks, beaches and historical areas such as St. Augustine.

25 ST. AUGUSTINE

When hurricane season ends on December 1, we relax and think more about enjoying our favorite places in Florida. One of our treasured local destinations that is especially pleasant in the late fall is St. Augustine. Located just 30 minutes south of Jacksonville on Florida's east coast, St. Augustine is known as "the nation's oldest city." After living in Florida for 20 years, we took the city's significance for granted. It wasn't until we helped my nephew with a school project that we fully explored the history and relevance of St. Augustine.

Professor jumped out of bed early on a Saturday morning in December. He was excited; we were taking Flat Stanley on a historical tour of St. Augustine including the Nights of Lights. Professor is always enthusiastic about sharing his passion for history so when my nephew sent his Flat Stanley to us, Professor planned to give Flat Stanley a complete tour.

"Who is Flat Stanley?" I asked when Professor opened the envelope and a cut-out piece of paper in the shape of a little boy fell out.

"*Flat Stanley* is based on the books written by Jeff Brown. In the original book, Flat Stanley is flattened by a bulletin board and then mailed to different places. In class, kids make their own Flat Stanley and send him on an adventure. Then the kids report back to the class. The purpose is to help kids get excited about reading and traveling."

I smiled broadly as I listened to Professor. A book which gets kids interested in reading and traveling is one that I fully support. "So, our plan is to take a walking tour of the historical areas of St. Augustine and photograph Flat Stanley at each location that we visit?"

"Yes," Professor said, gleefully. "It will be fun!"

"This includes staying for the Nights of Lights, when the city is ablaze with millions of white lights, right? I always enjoy seeing the lights this time of year."

Professor nodded, engrossed in his plan for a tour of the history of St. Augustine.

As we whirled around the house organizing snacks and backpacks for our day trip, Trouble barely paid attention. She curled up on the bed while stifling a few yawns, getting ready for a day of cat napping.

We arrived early in St. Augustine since the city is usually busy with tourists and the parking areas fill up quickly. We parked in the garage next to the St. Augustine & St. John's County Visitor Center and stopped in the Visitor Center to get a map. Although we knew our way around the city, we wanted to clearly document each historical place.

As we walked toward the historical part of the city, we passed the old graveyard next to the Visitor Center. One year, we took Dad on one of the guided ghost tours in St. Augustine and the tour stopped at this graveyard. I get chills each time I walk by the graveyard while thinking about the tales of past residents who purportedly haunt this area.

We took a photo of Flat Stanley by the old city gates on St. George Street. This historic cobblestone street is closed to vehicle traffic and lined with old buildings occupied by modern shops and restaurants. We stopped at Al's Pizza, an award-winning local restaurant, to eat a fresh-baked pizza while enjoying the view of the city, historical places and the St. Augustine inlet, from the second-floor deck.

As we ate our pizza, Professor offered a mini-lecture on the city's history. "St. Augustine was the first European colony in North America. The 'Old City' has a long and complex history beginning when the Spanish Conquistador Don Pedro Menendez de Aviles, founded the city in 1565. Menendez built a small fort and swept the French out of the area in order to claim it for Spain. The Spanish settled in for a long stay and in 1672 they started construction of a massive stone fort near the city gates, overlooking the harbor area."

From our viewpoint at Al's Pizza, we looked across at the fort – Castillo de San Marcos which is a National Monument. Professor continued with his history lecture. "Constructed of coquina limestone quarried in the nearby St. Augustine Beach area, the current fort and its predecessors have withstood numerous attacks and sieges. The most famous attack was led by English swashbuckler Sir Francis Drake, who with 2,000 men, attacked and plundered the city in 1586. The city and fortress were also attacked by English buccaneers in 1665 followed by sieges led by colonial governors of South Carolina and Georgia in 1702 and 1740."

"Okay, that's enough history for now." I held up one hand, interrupting Professor's lecture. I was anxious to do some shopping on St. George Street.

Professor gave me a wounded look, but nodded his head and waved at the waiter so we could pay the bill. After lunch, we wandered in and out of the shops on St. George Street. My routine includes stopping at Savannah Sweets for traditional Southern candy, including my favorite – pralines. We took Flat Stanley's photo inside the shop, gazing at the endless choices of chocolate-covered candies in the glass cases.

At the end of St. George Street, we turned right to go to the Government House Museum Visitor Center to learn more about the city. The museum includes pottery and other items which have been discovered in some of the archaeological excavations. Professor took this opportunity to continue his history lecture. He spoke in his sternest teacher's voice and a small crowd gathered around to listen to him.

"Where can we learn more about the city's history?" one person asked. Professor outlined a list of museums in the city.

"Can you tell us which beach to go to?" Professor and I rattled off a list of beaches in the St. Augustine area. We were fortunate to have so many choices including Anastasia State Park near the lighthouse.

"Where can we get ice cream?" I answered that question by directing everyone to the shops on St. George Street.

Finally, I grabbed Professor's arm and dragged him away from his fans. We needed to get to Flagler College for the afternoon tour. The tours only run twice a day so the afternoon tour was our last option. Tours are free, but a ticket is still required as tours are limited to 60 people. A few minutes later, we were sitting in the courtyard outside the entrance to Flagler College, enjoying the gardens and the unique architecture. We had walked by this building so many times but had never taken the tour. I knew the college was originally a hotel built by the railroad magnate Henry Flagler, but I didn't know the full history. Professor, of course, knew all about it.

"During the Gilded Age in the late 19th century, Henry Morrison Flagler, one of the founders of Standard Oil, became fabulously wealthy from the oil, railroad, and hotel businesses. He and his second wife visited St. Augustine in 1883, and decided it lacked facilities for tourists. In 1885, Flagler began construction of the Hotel Alcazar, an enormous hotel and casino for the period with 540 rooms. In order to bring travelers to his new hotel, he bought an existing railroad that ran through Jacksonville, Florida. Within two years, the hotel became extremely popular. Today the building houses the Lightner Museum and city offices."

I nodded my head in encouragement and Professor continued his speech. "Flagler went on to build other amazing Florida hotels that were world famous including the 'Breakers' in West Palm Beach and the Royal Palm in Miami. One of his most famous exploits was the completion of a railroad all the way to Key West, Florida in 1912. At the time, the over water railroad was one of the largest and most expensive engineering projects ever undertaken by a private citizen. Unfortunately, he was unable to enjoy it as he died from a fall at his Whitehall mansion in 1913."

Professor and I joined our group for the tour. Flagler also built the Ponce de Leon Hotel, which opened in 1888. The building was turned into Flagler College in the 20th century, but the elaborate architecture and interior design of the hotel remains. The tour of the college far exceeded my expectations; the inside of the building is ornate and exquisite in many places. Our tour guide was very knowledgeable, giving full responses to each question asked by the people in our group.

The most interesting room was the dining room with its 79 Tiffany stained-glass windows. I imagined the room filled with well-dressed wealthy people during the peak of the Gilded Age. The tour included the women's lounge. The room includes historical paintings and re-creations of 19th century ball gowns. Our tour guide explained how women were cloistered in the hotel, expected to remain behind closed doors while their husbands went out to the city for entertainment.

"Sounds like a good arrangement to me," Professor joked. He winced as I elbowed him in the ribs.

As the Flagler College tour ended, it was getting dark and time for us to walk around and see all of the lights. From the end of November through the end of January, St. Augustine glows with three million lights. Every building, tree, lamp post and anything else that can be wrapped with a strand of lights, is outlined in brilliant white lights. It's magical. The lights were just coming on as we entered the main square, Plaza de la Constitucion. The giant Christmas tree was lit so we took a picture of Flat Stanley standing on a branch of the tree. There was a line of children waiting to sit on Santa's lap next to the tree.

For us, looking at the lights of St. Augustine at Christmas time is an annual tradition. As we stood in the square, we talked about the darker side of St. Augustine's history. St. Augustine played a key role in the Civil Rights Movement in the 1960's. The city was a stronghold of white supremacists and the Klu Klux Klan (KKK). In 1964, Martin Luther King Jr., visited the city to bring attention to the plight of its black citizens. Violent clashes ensued with the KKK and others. In one incident, a local hotel owner threw acid on black swimmers in a hotel pool which was designated for guests with white skin. Ultimately, through the efforts of King and his associates, the city was desegregated. This history is acknowledged in the square with statues and memorials.

We continued walking through the square and crossed A1A to the Bridge of Lions, now outlined in bright white lights. We took Flat Stanley's photo next to one of the large stone lions that guard the bridge over the St. Augustine Inlet. Suddenly, we realized that the couple next to us was doing the same thing – taking photos of a Flat Stanley. We introduced ourselves and then introduced our Flat Stanleys. We took a picture of the two Flat Stanley characters, one from Pennsylvania and one from Ohio, standing on the railing with the Bridge of Lions in the background. We laughed about our Flat Stanley tours and marveled at the strange coincidence that we would meet in this spot.

Professor and I strolled on the walkway next to the inlet, enjoying the breeze blowing over the water. We had an awesome view of the lights outlining the historic buildings across from the inlet.

We ended our tour at Fort Castillo de San Marcos. We had toured the fort in the past, so we took a photo of Flat Stanley by the main entrance. Flat Stanley waved "Good-bye" to St. Augustine and we drove home.

When we arrived home, Trouble greeted us at the door. We tried to get a photo of her with Flat Stanley, but she swatted at Flat Stanley and would have torn him to shreds if I had not pulled him away quickly.

As we ate dinner, we reminisced about past Christmas holidays including the years when Grandma was still with us. Grandma always made Christmas very special. Christmas with Grandma was a scene from a storybook and we enjoyed all of the traditional family Christmas rituals. On Christmas Eve, we would have a big dinner with all of the traditional side dishes – mashed potatoes, sweet potato casserole, green beans and rolls. Mom's apple pie, homemade from apples that we picked in October, was dessert. Later in the evening, we gathered around the Christmas tree, feeling relaxed and peaceful. Grandma would read the Christmas story from the Bible and then we would each open one present.

Grandma's presents were special and best saved for Christmas day. Grandma worked in B. Altman's department store in the silver department. Every year we would get a special gift from her, wrapped in the B. Altman's shiny red gift boxes. I still have some of those gifts; they are treasures.

Christmas with Grandma was more than just special gifts. Grandma was a genuinely happy person – kind and loving in her selfless manner. She always worried about other people – never about herself. I always took great care to select just the right gift for Grandma, but it didn't really matter. I could have wrapped up a rock and given it to her. She would have opened it and said, "What a nice rock!" and then given me a big hug. Grandma was always spreading her loving kindness with big hugs.

So, as Professor and I ate brunch on Christmas morning, I felt melancholy, missing Grandma. Trouble perched on top of a wrapped gift sitting under the Christmas tree and looked at me as if she was trying to cheer me up. We took her photo and then she jumped up in my lap. I'm certain that this cat senses my moods and tries to help me. As I stroked her fur and scratched behind her ears, I gradually felt better.

AFTERWORD

On a chilly New Year's Eve, with temperatures close to freezing and a forecast for a heavy frost, Professor and I sat quietly in the living room. Trouble was sleeping, curled up next to me on a brown, fuzzy blanket on the couch.

At the end of the year, Professor and I like to talk about the previous 12 months, discussing the things we enjoyed and the challenges we had to overcome. We were looking at a map of the United States with pictures of cat paws showing our routes from Florida to Montana and back. We eventually decided to include the map at the beginning of this book as a visual overview of our travels with our cat.

Always philosophical, Professor likes to make profound statements on New Year's Eve. "We would never have driven across the country from Florida to Montana if we did not have the cat. We would have flown from Jacksonville to Bozeman. If we had flown to Bozeman, we would not have visited all of the so-called Fly Over States." Professor pointed to the Midwestern portion of the United States. He made the map on his computer and was admiring his work.

"You're right. We would have missed out on the opportunity to explore some neat places in Iowa, South Dakota and Wyoming. We would not have met so many wonderful people." Pictures of these places flashed through my mind.

Professor was still staring at the map, contemplating the full impact of our six trips across the United States with our cat. "The media paints our country as deeply divided – red and blue, black and white, conservative and liberal – lots of different labels. Our experience has been different. Everywhere we went from Florida to Montana we met kind people: people who stopped what they were doing to help us; people who smiled and said 'have a great trip'; people who were proud of where they lived and shared it with us."

I nodded my head. "Very true; people are just people, not a bunch of labels. We have had an amazing adventure traveling across the country and we would not have had the experience if we didn't have Trouble." The cat's ears twitched at the sound of her name. She opened her eyes halfway, to see why I was calling her name. When she realized that it didn't involve food, play time or snuggling, she went back to sleep.

Professor pointed to the Western coast of the U.S. and the Southwestern states. "We haven't really explored this part of the country. We have been to the Grand Canyon, Yosemite National Park, Arches National Park and Zion National Park, but there are many more places to visit in the West."

As much as I wanted to see some of the Western states, the drive from Florida to the West Coast, from Atlantic Ocean to Pacific Ocean, would be a very long drive – much longer than the drive to Montana. I scowled while trying to think about driving coast to coast with the cat. I just couldn't imagine it. "It's too hard to explore the West when we live in Florida," I said.

"Well, if we lived out West it would be easier." Professor spoke slowly, and I could see he had been thinking about this idea for some time.

"If we lived out West," I echoed, trying to absorb the idea.

Professor smiled – an unusually large smile. "Maybe we should move to Montana."

ACKNOWLEDGMENTS

Writing a book takes time and patience; in this case, mostly other people's patience with the writer's temperament. I would like to thank Professor for his kindness, love and understanding during our travels and while I was working on this project. My family reviewed early drafts and provided feedback. Their support of my storytelling and walks down memory lane helped me to flesh out some of my memories. My sisters spent valuable time editing the book. I could not have finished this project without their help. Trouble, of course, has been my constant companion since she first showed up in our garden. Some might say, "She's only a cat," but to us she is very special. I could not have written this book without her.

ABOUT THE AUTHOR

Ginnie L. Hansen is a writer, editor, and teacher. Ginnie L. Hansen lives in the Gallatin Valley in Montana with her husband and precocious cat, Trouble. When she is not writing books, she enjoys traveling and hiking in the Rocky Mountains. Read more about Ginnie and Trouble at www.the30000milecat.com.

We hope you have enjoyed the 30,000 Mile Cat Book 1

Reviews are important for independent books. We would greatly appreciate it if you would post a review on Amazon.com.

Printed in Great Britain
by Amazon

15160119R00088